Jesus Consumer

Reframing the Debate between Faith and Consumption

Michael L. Klassen

University Press of America,® Inc.
Lanham • Boulder • New York • Toronto • Plymouth, UK

Copyright © 2014 by University Press of America,® Inc.
4501 Forbes Boulevard, Suite 200, Lanham, Maryland 20706
UPA Aquisitions Department (301) 459-3366

10 Thornbury Road, Plymouth PL6 7PP, United Kingdom

All rights reserved

British Library Cataloguing in Publication Information Available

Library of Congress Control Number: 2013932367
ISBN: 978-0-7618-5633-7 (paperbound : alk. paper)—ISBN: 978-0-7618-5634-4 (electronic)

Cover photograph: *Jesus Leads the Gay Parade* by Robb Klassen, Paris 2007.
www.robbklassen.com

In Memory of Bennie Klassen (1926-2010)—loving father, respected business leader, happiest when he was with his customers and family.

Dedicated to Al Dueck and Richard J. Harris—mentors, beloved and inspiring professors—thank you so much!

The consumer revolution is a strange chapter in the ethnographic history of species. For what may have been the first time in history, a human community willingly harbored a nonreligious agent of social change, and permitted it to transform on a continual and systematic basis virtually every feature of social life. (McCracken 1987, p. 30)

Contents

Prologue		ix
Introduction: What do monks do when they aren't praying?		xv
1	Jesus Landlord: If Jesus was a carpenter, why didn't he build something?	1
2	Jesus Amish: What part of "own no property" don't we get?	13
3	Jesus Contractor: Are some cars more Christian than others?	27
4	Jesus Espresso: Does a "double skinny, half-caf" hold life's meaning?	45
5	Jesus Corporate: What's the difference between St. Joe's and Joe's Bar?	57
Conclusion		79
Notes		81
References		91
About the Author		95

Prologue

Eighty years ago, a well-known religious antagonist raised a question that has yet to be addressed. No longer!

> (Religion) has ruled human society for many thousands of years and has had time to show what it can achieve. If it had succeeded in making the majority of humankind happy, in comforting them, in reconciling them to life and in making them into vehicles of civilizations, no one would dream of altering the existing conditions. But what do we see instead? (Sigmund Freud, *The Future of an Illusion*, 1927,. p. 60)

What, indeed? Every Sunday morning the church congregation in your neighborhood has yet another opportunity to, as Freud writes, "Show what it can achieve."[1] Churches are diverse in their memberships, worship forms, and missions, but the Sunday morning experience can be distilled to an experience shared by most and one we may characterize as a type of consumer transaction. It involves two parties—one preacher and a raft of listeners—and an approximately one-hour encounter in which the first party attempts to convince the second to adopt the ideas he/she is proposing, ideas gleaned from his/her reading of the Church's holy writings. Here's how the deal goes down at First Pedestrian Church:

Pastor Shawn (fictitious), adorned in priestly regalia and armed with commentaries by exceptionally bright people, stands up, holds forth, and hopes to wax eloquent. He preaches. And in so doing he gives concrete expression to abstract ideas—ancient ideas that Jesus had. Pastor Shawn pitches an idea and Shelley (in attendance), might catch it. But, as one who had devoted the better part of his career speaking before groups of people, she probably won't. The reason Shelley does not enthusiastically adopt and apply Pastor Shawn's instruction to her life has nothing to do with her lack of understanding, religious disbelief, or attentiveness. Rather, it has to do with her relative inability to *literally* apply Shawn's directives (and by extension, Jesus' teachings) to her life. By this, I mean that Shelley's first order of business is to learn something that will make her life more efficient and useful, if not meaningful. In other words, Shelley's desire to get Jesus' words to "make sense" for her life overshadows her desire to get them "right" (i.e., correct).

Psychologist Steven Pinkner says it well: "The human brain is made for fitness, not truth."

Shelley's "reconstructive" response to Pastor Shawn is not unique. She does this with every piece of information she receives, whether it comes from her boyfriend, her mother, or her boss. Like taking possession of an apartment, Shelley transforms the "property of instruction" temporarily leased to her by her pastor, handling and manipulating it. Silently reading into the sermon the landscapes of her childhood, her life, her career, her accomplishments, and her disappointments, Shelley insinuates and creates her own take on the message that is vastly different than the one Pastor Shawn intended, or could have ever imagined. She slips into a place the Shawn thought he had secured—Shelley's is not a case of inattention but fabrication. Why does she veer so far off course?

If we could magically get into Shelley's brain we would see a process taking place called, "the consumption of ideas." She has taken possession of a set of ideas, compliments of Pastor Shawn—much like she takes a baguette, some shavings of mozzarella cheese, a couple of Roma tomatoes, and a bottle of olive oil—and has created something helpful for accomplishing her objectives and meeting her personal needs and wants. As Shawn speaks, Shelly adds to the pot a little of this, subtracting a lot of that, and eventually arrives at a "flavor" that conform to her self-concept, how she hopes to be seen by others, her goals and plans, her mood at the time, her psychological idiosyncrasies, and her privately-held bigotries and personal biases. (Freud would love this, wouldn't he?)

The result: What Shelley ultimately concludes about what Pastor Shawn instructs may be as far away from his intended message as a Plymouth Voyager is from a Porsche Carrera.

In all fairness, Pastor Shawn has good intentions. Having been a pastor myself, I can say without any doubt that the vast majority of men and women who choose to become Christian pastors sincerely want to change people's lives and the world for the better, and that they believe that the methods and techniques for such change may be discovered through personal spiritual conversion, the discipline of prayer, the study of holy writings, and a deep mindfulness about the pickles they and members of their faith community get themselves into.[2] We can think of it like this:

Every Sunday Pastor Shawn—like hundreds of pastors worldwide—generously, eagerly, offers Shelley a thoroughly clean, freshly painted, sparkling white "apartment of ideas," a place to consume extraordinary principles, ideas, and dreams. What he often fails to foresee is what Shelley will do with his words, how Shelley will cover the clean, white apartment he offers her with curly cues, swirls, and a rainbow of colors that conform to her personal liking. What Pastor Shawn would do well to understand is that, what members of his audience do with a religious idea is the same thing they do with a two dollar can of air freshener—they acquire it, use it to accomplish their personal goals and ambitions, and eventually, they divest themselves of it, exchanging it for another useful idea to construct new meaning. So...

WHAT WOULD GLADE AIR FRESHENER DO?

Here's what the people at Glade have learned that Pastor Shawn may benefit by knowing: that 99.9% of the consumers occupying the air freshener universe are not interested in the "place-ness" but the "space-ness" of their products, services, and ideas. That the physicality of their aerosols, candles and those annoying gadgets that squirt at you when you enter a public toilet—their ingredients, components, and functional characteristics play second fiddle to the psychological and social experience of consuming Glade products—their smells, how they make the users feel, the security they provide homeowners anticipating the arrival of guests, and so on. And this is what we may, by extension, conclude about First Pedestrian Church, its pastor and its parishioners: that for 99.9% of the Sunday morning assembly, the ingredients of a sermon—its theological approximation to the truth, it historical accuracy, and its consistency with denominational beliefs—don't hold a scented candle to the importance ascribed by one and all to the personal experience of consuming the ideas of a sermon—ideas that affect how parishioners and the pastor himself feels, the emotional security they experience, and the positive reinforcement of their own behavior (sinful or otherwise) that it offers. In short: *Humans consume religion*—its services, products and ideas—taking what they want, ignoring the rest, looking for the next opportunity, maneuvering as they go along. Most of Pastor Shawn's listeners use Jesus' ideas and his interpretation of them in much the same way that they use an air freshener: to freshen things up a bit.

WAS JESUS ANY DIFFERENT?

How does Jesus feel about this? Some (particularly pastors who have a sneaking feeling that their congregants aren't listening carefully) believe that Jesus hates this kind of thing, insisting that this type of posturing, insinuation, and "reading into" is precisely the kind of behavior that Christians need to confess as sinful. Pastors often share the salesperson's disgust when their customer claims that he is entitled to an experience of the product that was never promised and cannot be guaranteed. The truth is, pastors hate this kind of thing, but Jesus *loves* it. It reminds him of his own life, of how he responded to the "Pastor Shawn's" of his day.

To better understand Jesus' own response to religious ideas offered to him, we raise a provocative question: "Was Jesus a good religious person?"

The question of Jesus and his religion is really a question about Jesus and Judaism, not Christianity, and we sharpen the question above when we restate it: "Was Jesus a good Jew?"[3] Christians' intent on showing the connection between Jesus and the promised Messiah of the God of Abraham are likely to answer in the affirmative. But what about Jewish people who have no vested interest in making such an association? If you want to know whether or not Jesus was a good Jew, well, why not ask a good Jew? In his explanation of *Why the Jews Rejected Jesus* (the title of his book), Jewish writer David Klinghoffer pulls no punches about what he thinks about Jesus and his practice of Judaism. Klinghoffer thinks that Jesus was lousy at being a Jew, and he argues that the reasons Jesus was held in such low regard by his Jewish counterparts (and, by implication, could not possibly have been the Messiah) were first, because of his disregard for the Jewish holy writ (Torah), and second, because of his disrespect for the Jewish religious leaders of this day. Klinghoffer's views aren't exclusively his or his Jewish peers. Christian theologian, James Carroll (2001) concurs with Klinghoffer's argument (albeit not his conclusions about Jesus' Messiahship) pointing out that many of the Jewish practices Jesus ignored were central Jewish tenets, not unimportant directives but sacred Law taken directly from the Torah and taught for centuries as coming directly from Yahweh. So is Klinghoffer correct when he asserts that Jesus wasn't very religious, or at least not religious enough to be considered a good Jew?

Klinghoffer is both right *and* wrong when he asserts that Jesus was not a very good Jew. He is *right* in believing that Jesus was not religious enough to be a good Jew, and we can be confident about this because of the confidence Jesus showed in his rejection of the offers extended to him by the Jewish leaders. If Jesus had wanted to be a good Jew, he had every opportunity. But, as we know, religion's representatives, its *"landlords,"* (a term I explain later) were never able to keep Jesus in line with the party line. These men weren't ogres, nor were they stingy with the things they had to offer Jesus. We sometimes overlook the friendly banter between Jesus and the Jewish authorities, particularly members of the Sanhedrin (cf. Trueblood, 1964), preferring rather to paint the two parties in broad black and white strokes, bad guys versus the good guy, crafty salesmen versus the unsuspecting buyer. What the religious leaders of his day offered Jesus (like what Pastor Shawn offers his parishioners) was actually fairly impressive: a corpus of ancient and tested ideas, goals, and vetted principles, an "apartment" with freshly-painted walls, turn-key ready! So what kept Jesus from signing a lease with these landlords? Simply put, Jesus made it clear by his words and action that he did not intend to completely follow the terms of their lease. The religious leaders of his day set down stringent parameters, some taken directly from the Torah and some of their own making, and before they would work with Jesus they insisted that he must first sign off on their terms, agreements that would restrict what he may and may not do once he agreed to rent from them. Jesus was allowed to stay in religion's apartments *as long as* he did not change a thing, as long as he didn't paint the walls or hang some pictures. We know that Jesus rejected the offer and its terms, but do we know why? Jesus—like us and like Shelley—was born to create, to actively consume, not passively receive, and active consumption, along with a bundle of other human compulsions, is something the Jewish leaders could not tolerate. Many Christian leaders are not particularly keen on the idea either. In fact, we will read later, that entire Christian traditions have formed over the centuries that have based their very existence on following Jesus' consumer teachings in a far more strict and literal way than Jesus followed his own Jewish consumer teachings. Ironically, millions of believers have chosen a course with their Christianity that Jesus consciously and deliberately rejected with his own personal religion. This leads to my next point:

Klinghoffer is *wrong* about Jesus when he writes that he did not take his Judaism seriously. All indications from the New Testament record indicate that Jesus was a devout, strictly monotheistic Jew who understood the Holy Scriptures, followed most of them, spent time in the Temple, and so forth. Jesus took his Jewish faith very seriously; he just didn't take all of its teachings completely *literally*. Like Shelley, he elected to create something new and different with religious ideas, many of which, like old musty rooms, needed a good freshening up. And this refusal on his part coupled with his inclination to apply imaginative twists to seemingly unbendable Jewish law, is what contributed to his being thrown into conflict with some of his Jewish counterparts for whom faithfulness was equated with a strict application of ancient laws. Interestingly enough, most of the laws that stood at the heart of the conflict between Jesus and the Jewish leaders had to do with consumer practices—what one could eat, what one could wear, and so forth. I argue here that the struggle between Jesus and the Jews of his day over what were essentially consumption laws was a defining one, setting the boundaries between centuries-old Judaism and the brand new "Jesus movement," delineating the differences between how adherents of both groups would carry out God's purpose in the consumer habits and rituals of their daily lives, how they would conduct the practice of *their* everyday lives.

We know how the story ends. Disgusted, Jesus told his own followers who were hoping to find a nice place to hole up for a while not to waste their time with the religious leaders, or, for that matter, any landlord, Roman landlords included, that required them to sign a contract that included a clause that stated: "renters may not change a thing in our apartments"—that required them to deny their basic human need to change, create, imagine, and actively consume. Jesus understood that a strict and literal application of religious instruction to a person's life with no room for personal interpretation was both an extraordinary and unreasonable demand to put on human beings created in the image of their divine creator. While he didn't use these very words, Jesus understood that people, at heart, are consumers, beings that actively engage the object of their consumption, whether that object is a religious belief or a dish in need of more pepper and a few spices. In short, by his example and teachings Jesus encouraged his followers to follow their human inclination to change things, shake things up, manipulate, construct, taste, chew, try on, and throw in an extra spice or two—consume with abandon! But how—how to move the latest generation in a centuries-old religion, his generation, away from consumer practices that they and their ancestors had been taught were critical to successfully winning God's favor?

To help his followers keep their nerve and not accept attractive offers from Jewish and Roman landlords, Jesus focused people's attention on a single truth: landlords are only as powerful as renters permit them to be. He understood, as we do, that the power of the powers-that-be rests on the cooperation of their consumers. Whether it is Harry's Hardware or a billion-dollar financier like Bears Stearns, when the consumer bails, the gig is up. This idea—consumer-based, transactional in nature, and descriptive of how Jesus wanted his followers to conduct their daily affairs—threw Jesus and later, the Church, into deadly conflict with the Jewish and Roman landlords of their day who suspected that if people started taking Jesus seriously, their gig was up. Jesus' unwillingness to adhere to a literal interpretation of their beliefs about consumption—the proper way to eat, what to eat, what to wear, how to pray, and so forth—cost him his very life. His life and death set an example for consumer followers through the ages: do business with the landlords who think they understand exactly what it is God literally requires and life will be smooth, albeit a creative wasteland, tedious, and supremely monotonous. Choose Jesus and prepare for a life of material surprise and immaterial abundance.

Introduction

What do monks do when they aren't praying?

A short distance from our family home is a fully-operating Trappist monastery. Visiting the brothers (monks) who reside here is like stepping back to the sixth century when the "The Rule of St. Benedict," a guide that describes the Order's values and ideals, was written. Many people—Christians and non-believers, alike—come to the monastery for retreats and personal reflection. Once, while paying a short visit to the monastery with our elementary-aged children, we had dinner served by the brothers, which consisted of homemade soup, fresh fruit, and hard-crusted bread. I could tell that my seven-year-old son was fascinated with the men who served us, dressed in the robes of their founders. Shortly after dinner, there was a call to evening prayers and our family and other guests proceeded to the chapel, a tall, slender Gothic structure focusing on the altar, lined on one side with icons and candles, and on the other, hooded monks chanting centuries-old prayers. After the short service, I told my son that this prayer service was not the first one the brothers had attended that day, but that the men who lived in the monastery had dedicated their lives to praying every two hours, round the clock, for the rest of their lives. My son thought quietly, trying to comprehend a lifestyle that must have seemed like a nightmare to a seven-year-old boy. His question after a prolonged period of silence caught me off guard: "What do they do in the meantime?" To maintain their unique ministry, the monks, all of whom have taken vows of poverty, run a profitable casket construction business. There is no mystery here: what monks, and what you and I do "in the meantime," is the same thing: we consume.[1]

The purpose in writing this book is to argue the case that Jesus of Nazareth—a first-century peasant who lived his life without trade, money, property, or the means or interest to defend himself and the little he owned—was a consummate consumer who displayed an unflappable confidence in the expressive power of the material world to bring about personal and social change. How have people responded to Jesus' consumption teachings articulated in his so-called "mission instructions," and recorded in the tenth chapter of the Gospels of Matthew and Luke? In three ways: A relatively small group have decided that to take seriously these centuries-old teachings means they must be taken literally (a stance adopted by the earliest Christians and, to this day, by many conservative Christian sects and some anti-consumerism groups); an even smaller group of people, most notably biblical and historical scholars, have understood these teachings as ancient relics, applicable to primitive people but not to modern-day consumers; and the rest, the majority, have simply thrown their hands up in frustration: "Surely Jesus didn't mean for us to live this way—or did he?" Here I present a fourth response that argues that, in order for people to exploit the full power of their goods in a modern consumer culture, they must go beyond seeing their possessions as purely instrumental means to ends and use them, instead, to consciously and thoughtfully express their most deeply held beliefs and values. I base this position and my defense of it primarily on Jesus' teachings, but also I build support on the findings of modern business and social research as well as the experiences gleaned from seven years as a Mennonite seminarian and pastor and over twenty years of experience as an advertising consultant and business professor.

WHY FOCUS ON CONSUMPTION?

Consumption is as natural and ubiquitous as breathing—every living creature does it. And yet, today, even as Americans accrue direct material, social, and psychological benefits from living in one of the most sophisticated consumer cultures the world has ever seen, they are uneasy about consumption, especially when it comes to their own brand of consumer behavior and culture. Many Americans, especially American Christians, are apt to associate consumerism with the dark rather than the bright side of international trade agreements, free market capitalism, and wealth creation. Are these attitudes justified, or is it time for conscientious people of faith to stop worrying and start learning to love their stock portfolios?

While I use mostly scholarly material to construct my argument for consumerism here, early experiences from growing up in a family business also inform my writing. One incident in particular from the fall of 1962 stands out. The family I grew up in was devoutly Christian and most members of my extended family—a first-generation Russian immigrant family of uncles, aunts, and a slew of cousins—spent six days a week working in the business begun by my grandfather and a portion of the seventh day in church. One Sunday, after listening to a particularly pointed sermon about the sins of Christmas commercialism, family members gathered (more quietly than usual) at my parent's home for Sunday dinner. This wasn't the first time we had heard such anti-business discourse. Each time the criticism stung and raised uncertainty for us about the vocation our family had chosen. The patriarch of our family, Grandpa Gerhard, had come to the U.S. in the early 1920's with less than a dollar in his pocket, fleeing the Communist regime in the U.S.S.R. with five children, a wife ill with typhoid (who died shortly after the family's arrival in the U.S.), and fewer than four crates containing all his earthly possessions. Having lost nearly everything and been lined up twice before a Red Army firing squad, Grandpa fled Russia to save himself from certain death and search for a better life.[2] By the 1950s he had finally managed to accrue a measure of business and financial success. A product of the American Dream, how could he and we, his offspring, take seriously the Sunday sermon and continue to carry on our commercial enterprises? How could we be successful business people *and* good Christians?

After the meal, family members gathered in front of the T.V. to watch football and doze, taking time to catch up on some rest.[3] Halftime was interrupted by a news break announcing that retail sales were up for the season and that consumer spending was as strong as the country had seen in a decade.[4] The cloud of doubt and guilt that had hung over our Sunday meal was suddenly lifted. As if on cue, my father and his brothers started clapping and shaking hands (high-fives had not been invented yet). All were in a holiday mood—all except my Aunt Linda, who was a particularly strict Christian. She surveyed the merriment, clucked her tongue, and walked out of the room.

My aunt's discomfort with commercial success is shared by millions of Americans, many of whom have directly benefited from our system of business. Historian Peter N. Stearnes (2006, p. 67), states that in the U.S. consumerism has "picked up traditional Christians themes of ... greed, gluttony, (and the pursuit of) false gods." Christian leaders often lead the chorus of criticism against business, and today, popular Christian writers, such as Jim Wallis and Rick Warren, and even a former U.S. President, Jimmy Carter, argue that Jesus' message to humanity is underscored by strong anti-consumption teachings. Catholics, Protestants, Evangelicals, Charismatic Christians, tiny congregations, and mega-churches—many stand ready to castigate American consumers for their over-consumption and overspending. Little has changed since 1962: America's business community, perceived to be overly ambitious, greedy, and morally suspect, often take the brunt of the Church's criticism, while America's middle-and lower-class consumers are held up as the hapless victims of a self-absorbed and greedy consumer culture gone wild. What do we stand to lose by painting a picture of faith and consumption in such bold strokes of black and white?

Here I explain why I believe that the Church's judgmental stance toward consumerism is not only seriously disconnected from the consumer experiences of most American Christians, but also why an overly negative Christian position contradicts the very heart of Jesus' teachings. Using Jesus' life and words, I build support for the ideas that consumerism has as much capacity to benefit people as to harm them, to contribute to society as to undermine its basic values, and to enhance social relationships as to detract from them. I am not acting merely as a cheerleader for American capitalism, nor am I naïve about the deleterious impact of consumer culture on its members. Along with being a businessperson I was also a Christian minister for five years, and I have spent countless hours discussing with friends and colleagues the effect of American consumerism (even if that specific term was not used) on their lives. I have seen firsthand how consumer culture injects its citizens with unethical and immoral values (a "hypodermic" model of consumption, if you will). But here I do not participate in this longwinded and, in my opinion, overwrought discussion. Instead, I build support for the positive role of one's possessions, and I demonstrate how goods and property act as instruments of imaginative construction, frequently in a manner that is positive, innovative, and even personally transformational. My favorable bias toward consumerism rests on four things:

1. Consumer and psychological research that support the idea of human beings as attentive and thoughtful creators, not dupes or automatons (e.g., James 1890).
2. A cognitive psychological understanding of human nature as primarily constructive (e.g., Bruner and Goodman 1947) emotional (e.g., Izard, et al 1984), and relational (e.g., Combs and Snygg 1949).
3. Consumer research that understands goods as more than means to ends and as objects we commonly use symbolically to express our deepest convictions (e.g., Belk, et al. 1989).
4. Recent research on the teachings and behavior of Jesus (e.g., Crossan, 1991) that paint a fresh, new, and sometimes counter-intuitive interpretation of Jesus and his teachings.

There is a fifth reason for my positive attitude towards consumerism that has no apparent connection to biblical instruction or the individual's spiritual quest, but whose effect on America's rich and poor is profound and unprecedented in the history of humankind.

HOW DO JESUS' AND OUR UNDERSTANDING OF INCOME AND CONSUMPTION DIFFER?

In Jesus' world, the economic realities you and I take for granted did not exist and, as we will eventually read, could not have existed. Consequently, I believe that to simply apply Jesus' teachings literally in modern consumer economies and cultures runs the risk of misinterpretation and seriously deflate their impact. A visit to the mall clarifies how Jesus' and our experience of income and consumption are very different:

My father, now retired, once remarked while the two of us were walking through a shopping mall over a Christmas break home from college: "It's a shame you can't tell who's rich and poor anymore." I asked him what he meant. He replied: "See that man over there." He pointed in the direction of an older man dressed in a pair of beat-up running shoes, ill-fitting jogging pants, and a coffee stained t-shirt. "I've done business with him for years. He's a multi-millionaire but the way he's dressed, it looks like he can barely afford to eat." "In the old days," Dad continued, "he wouldn't have been caught dead looking like that in public." I recalled that I never once saw my grandfather without a suit and tie. I even remember seeing him one time wearing a jacket, vest, gold watch, polished Oxfords and silk tie while gardening!

Business researchers have a name for my father's observation: "the blurring of consumer symbols," by which they mean that what once symbolized wealth and success no longer holds such meaning. One business writer puts it this way: "Order a pair of Guggi loafers and the delivery boy might very well be wearing his own pair."[5] Researchers are pretty sure they know what has brought about these changes. The blurring phenomenon has come about as high priced brands, such as Armani and Mercedes Benz, have, with the help of cheap foreign labor and reduced trade restrictions, created cheaper products (referred to as "bridge items") to stay competitive with the likes of American Eagle and Kia Motors. Now, even America's poorest can consume products once reserved only for the rich; now, Americas' rich can "slum" at a local mall without a tinge of embarrassment. (Imagine, for instance, Andrew Carnegie or Henry Ford, Sr. appearing before an international forum in Khaki pants, an open-collared shirt in bad need of ironing, and running shoes—standard fare for Bill Gates and many of today's newly minted billionaires.) The boundary between what the rich and poor consume cuts both ways. In the last month I have witnessed a private limousine pulling up to a McDonald's drive-up window, a $150,000 Bentley convertible parked at Wal-Mart, a homeless man inquiring as to whether or not the lettuce in his salad was organically grown, and a working class family of five trying to decide whether to spend their Christmas holiday skiing in the Rockies or cruising to Puerto Vallarta. Today, to adequately interpret and enact Jesus' consumer teachings, it is important for us to distinguish between a person's income and his level of consumption. In short, we need to differentiate between what a person makes and what he's likely to wear to the mall. So what precisely determines the quality of the material lives of modern consumers?

In Jesus' world, the money one made and the consumer goods he owned were closely related and I am suggesting that this relationship, absent in our own world, profoundly shaped Jesus' message and left a void of understanding for us moderns. What's different? First-century Galilee preceded the birth of MasterCard by some 1,900 years, and so in Jesus' day you owned what you could afford and you afforded (i.e., paid for) what you owned—otherwise, you wouldn't have the option to own it. In other words, during the time that Jesus lived and taught, income and consumption were directly and inextricably related. In Jesus' day, income was the single most important characteristic that determined a person's quality of life. In contrast, today, income and consumption share a loose and indirect relationship; indeed, U.S. income no longer plays the role it has for decades in determining how well a person lives. The figures bear this out. First, the bad news: The disparity in income between America's richest and poorest is as wide as ever. The average annual income of the richest Americans (just short of $150,000) and the poorest (just a little above $18,000) stands at a whopping 8.3 to 1 ratio. On the other hand, the difference between the annual household *consumption* of the rich ($22,500) and the poor $10,700) is a mere 2.1 to 1. And, the consumption per person for America's gargantuan middle class which consists of approximately 70% of the U.S. population is $13,800, which compared to America's lower class ($10,700) is practically the same (W. Michael Cox and Richard Alm, *New York Times:* "How Americans Spend their Money," Sunday February 10, 2008). If for Americans, income no longer plays the principle role in determining the quality of their material lives as it did in Jesus' day or even in their grandparents' days, then what does?

I'm sure many Americans shared my incredulity upon hearing a news report in August 2000 about a homeless man who, gaining free Internet access at his neighborhood library went from rags to riches after constructing his own Web business. This indigent entrepreneur acquired collectibles and used goods for pennies and sold them to consumers worldwide, realizing (according to my calculations) as much as 500% profit margins on some items. His ambition and ingenuity eventually permitted him to enter the middle class. This man succeeded not because of the size of his bank account, family connections, or property holdings, but because of his ability to gain easy and affordable access to the newest technological products and services—that and a healthy dose of ingenuity and imagination.[6]

This homeless person's accomplishments show us that in our world, unlike Jesus' world, *accessibility* is the key determinant in an individual's material success and quality of life. The consumer "playing field" is still not completely level but it is certainly not as bumpy as it was in Jesus' day. Easy access to technological and product innovations permeate all levels of social class, income, and education in the U.S. Today, my business students are privy to information that only the worlds' most powerful business and political leaders had access to when I started teaching in 1987, and most of that information costs pennies, (an annual $52 university computer fee, to be exact), not millions as it once did. While the pace of technological innovation since the last half of the twentieth-century has been impressive, the diffusion of innovation in the U.S. and its impact on the American consumer over the last three decades has been nothing short of breathtaking. In large part this is due to the affordability (a critical but not essential determinant of accessibility) of so many of today's latest innovations. Consider that in 1984, *at the average wage*, an American consumer needed to put in 435 hours of work time to afford a personal computer. Today, he can buy his own PC after a little more than a half a week's work, or about 25 hours. In 1984, to own a cell phone required 10 weeks of work (456 hours). Today, one can buy his own cell phone with the wages accrued before his lunch break (4 hours).

Income disparity or consumption parity—what would focus Jesus' attention if he were to launch his ministry today? Jesus was aware of, even resigned to, the income differences between the rich and the poor. His statement indicating that the poor would always be present is just as true today as it was then (The Gospel of Mark 14: 7). Still, one wonders, how would Jesus respond to the relative lack of differences between the rich, middle class, and poor that we observe in today's economically developed countries with respect to personal and household consumption? Would he bother telling a story about a beggar picking up scraps under a rich man's table before an American audience who may observe, as I did a few weeks ago, a modern-day beggar (i.e., a homeless man) sipping on a $5 cappuccino in front of Starbucks? I have to believe that even Jesus would do a double-take watching two families at table aboard a Caribbean cruise—one middle class and other living near the poverty line—discussing the finer qualities of the lobster bisque. [Don't believe such a discussion would ever take place? More than 44% of cruise passengers make between $25,000 (which is less than $4,000 above the official poverty line) and $60,000 per year (just a little above the average salary for lower middle-class Americans), according to cruise-information-center.com.].[7] Conscientious Americans, like Jesus, should be disturbed by the income disparity between the world's rich and the poor, but as important as this is ....well, another book, another time. Here, we focus on consumption. How would Jesus have us consume? We begin with a fundamental question:

WHAT, PRECISELY, IS CONSUMPTION?

My definition of consumption is built on four quotations—none from Donald Trump, Stephen Covey, or Robert Kiyosaki, or for that matter, any best-selling business guru. The first three quotes are from the French philosopher Michel de Certeau (1984) and the last from the renowned, twentieth-century Protestant theologian, H. Richard Niebuhr. Why these two writers? The importance of Niebuhr's work, particularly his book, *Christ and Culture* (1952), for clarifying the delicate relationship between the Christian believer and his resident culture cannot be overemphasized. John G. Stackhouse, Jr. writes in his review in *Christianity Today*, (April 22, 2002) that *Christ and Culture* was "one of the most influential Christian books of the past century. Perhaps no other book has dominated an entire theological conversation for so long."[8] Niebuhr provides a broad and theoretical understanding of a central theme of this book, namely, the relationship between Jesus' followers and their resident culture. What de Certeau contributes to the discussion here is more specific to consumer behavior and attitudes. A French Jesuit and a distinguished scholar in his own right who stood shoulder-to-shoulder with the likes of Foucault and Bourdieu, Michel de Certeau, is credited with conducting one of the most extensive studies of consumer behavior ever undertaken when, from 1974 -1978, he and a team of researchers examined the daily consumer behavior of the inhabitants of the Croix-Rousse neighborhood in the city of Lyons, France. His findings are published in a two-volume monograph titled, *The Practice of Everyday Life* (1980). Luce Girard's introduction to the study (p. xxxv) asserts that among those who have tried to explain consumer behavior over the decades, from economic philosophers to full-on marketers, de Certeau's method and conclusions stand apart. He writes "Where consumerism saw only the passive consumption of finished products, purchase volumes to be increased, or market shares moved ...where Marxist vocabulary spoke in terms of exploitation, of imposed behaviors and products, of mass culture and uniformity, Michel de Certeau proposed (the idea) of the creative activity of those in the *practice of the ordinary* (seeing it as his responsibility to identify the consumer's) 'ways of operating.'" (Emphasis mine) After four years, what did de Certeau's (1980) conclude?

"Consumer behavior is the practice of everyday living."

Appropriately, he titled his 400-page work: *The Practice of Everyday Life*. Many marketing experts concur with de Certeau's understanding of consumption. Now in its fourteenth edition, William Pride and O.C. Ferrell's *Marketing*, has been a standard textbook for countless marketing professionals and professional-in-training. Pride and Ferrell define consumer behavior as: *"the buying behavior of those who purchase products for personal or household use"* (Marketing, 14th edition, 2008, NY: Houghton Mifflin Company, 121). And, after over 20 years in the business classroom, here is my own definition: *"Consumer behavior explains why ordinary people do what they do in the marketplace."* Both definitions share an appreciation for the "un-sexy," mundane, and often, monotonous process people go through daily when they buy, consume, and divest themselves of products and services. De Certeau helps non-business people to understand something that marketing professionals have known for decades: that American's daily consumer behavior often has little or no relation to the things they normally associate with consumerism—things like T.V. commercials, Madison Avenue, consumer focus groups, mailing lists, and databases. It's much simpler than that. Consumerism is mostly concerned with the ways we operate in order to survive from one day to the next. Again, de Certeau (1980): "(Consumer behavior) consists of the collection of perishable creations that allow people to stay alive."

This last quote makes sense for America's homeless, and I would be the last person to minimize the singular goal of staying alive that stands at the heart of the daily consumer activities of countless millions, but can we honestly say that daily survival stands at the center of the behavior of America's middle class and affluent?" Yes, we can. In the U.S., household expenditures on transportation, housing, and food (i.e., the necessities) outpace consumers' purchases of clothing and entertainment (the non-necessities) as much as 7-to-1 (Cox and Alm, 2008). (And just in case we believe that for the American consumer it's all about me, me, and me, the same study also found that American's charitable contributions lapped their spending on luxury goods by a healthy 2-to-1 ratio.)

Admittedly, modern marketing practices are notorious for employing techniques designed to create consumer demands for things that are completely unnecessary for daily living. As a marketing professor, investor, and business consultant, I am periodically called upon to defend my career choice in the face of advertising manipulation and other marketing shenanigans. A recent encounter on a flight home after a business trip illustrates this. Making small talk with the passenger sitting next to me, the inevitable question finally came up: "What do you do for a living?" I hesitated, but finally replied: "I'm a marketing professor and I consult with businesses about their advertising." My companion's response was quick and thoughtless: "Oh, you're one of those guys who try to get us to buy things we don't need." In the last few years, I have advised my advertising students to answer stranger's questions about their career, simply: "I'm in business." It saves a lot of frustration.

Is that what's it's all about for American businesses, getting consumers to buy things they don't really need? Consider that in the U.S., which boasts the largest marketing industry in the world, the lion's share of product advertising and promotion is squarely directed at everyday consumer products designed to meet consumer needs, *not* wants. Billions of ad dollars (roughly 80% of all advertising in the U.S.) land in daily newspapers where promotions for local sales and deals on every day, non-luxury, consumer necessities—dish detergent, fresh produce, garden tools, office supplies, undergarments, toothpaste, pain relievers—dominate. While consumer practices may be seen in silvery jet liners, glass skyscrapers, and upscale shopping malls, we shouldn't forget that they are also on display in America's used clothing stores, sidewalk sales, and roadside markets. In these consumer spaces, discreet and largely unnoticed, resides the principle consumer architecture of ancient and modern societies, according to de Certeau (1980), who observes: "A society is ... composed of ...innumerable practices that remain 'minor.' It is in this ... silent reserve of procedures that we should look for 'consumer' practices."

While it is easy to focus on celebrity excesses and middle class Americans' inability to get enough of a good thing, de Certeau's intensive four-year study reveals what truly constitutes consumer behavior, namely, the seemingly insignificant habits, rituals, and routines of everyday life. The simple acts of brushing one's teeth, sipping a cup of tea, and taking one's kids to violin lessons—these are the "minor" practices where the vast majority of consumer activity is enacted in America and around the world. These, according to de Certeau are the heart and soul of every consumer culture, even consumer cultures as sophisticated as our own. And it is these practices that provide the framework as well as the direction for the analysis here. Why has the focus of Christian leaders and others been inordinately on greed, materialism and the dark side of capitalism? I believe that we are the recipients of too narrow a definition of consumption, an error that H. Richard Niebuhr (1951) warned against fifty years ago when he wrote: "It is fallacious to think of culture as purely materialistic."

Estee Lauder, famously said about her company: "We don't sell cosmetics; we sell hope." Consumption in modern societies involves the manipulation of material, to be sure, but it also involves, as this cosmetics queen implies, the manipulation of the *im*material—the symbolic expression of the things we own and conspicuously display. The writing of people like de Certeau and Niebuhr is foundational for consumer research conducted later in U.S. universities by people like the Canadian anthropologist, Grant McCracken (1988), and the University of Utah psychologist, Russell Belk (1985), who, along with marketing scholars Elizabeth Hirschman of Rutgers University and Morris Holbrook of Columbia University (1981) focused their research on "the consumption of goods as symbols." Today, corporate researchers are as likely to ask questions about product expression as product use, and marketing managers are apt to direct their examinations at product features and functions *as well as* the principles and ideas their products and services express.

WHAT DIRECTION IS TAKEN IN THIS BOOK?

Here, I use de Certeau and Niebuhr's work to examine the oft-overlooked immaterial effects and byproducts of material goods. This prompts me to ask several questions addressed later: How do material goods express immaterial ideas? What role do consumer objects play in articulating religious ideals and dreams? How did Jesus use the power of concrete, material goods to express abstract, lofty principles? Why has the Christian religion long insisted that its highest ideals remain hidden, removed from the nitty-gritty of people's daily material lives and transported to an ideal, immaterial location that is largely inaccessible to the common person? What have certain Christian denominations lost by equating faithful consumption solely with the *use* of goods, ignoring (even judging as sinful) the *expressive* potential of possessions? While the analysis here spans social research, from psychology to anthropology to modern marketing theory, it is self-evident that for a book like this one Jesus' life and teachings must provide the foundation for understanding how he intended for people to consume. And so we turn first to Jesus and his consumer instructions. Next, examining the Church's response, we discover that with the exception of a handful of Christians over the centuries, Jesus' consumer ideals have been largely ignored and/or seriously misconstrued. Finally, we examine the practice of what I call, "Consumptianity," which constitutes a new consumerist approach to understanding Jesus' teachings about our possessions.

Finally, on a personal note, I express humility as I ask you, the reader, to step into a rich stream (or perhaps, a minefield) of interpretation directed at one of the most significant persons to ever walk the face of the earth. You can appreciate that the task of re-framing an old debate necessarily will require, in this instance, a novel understanding of the principle player (i.e. Jesus of Nazareth) and his core beliefs, including his most self-defining attitudes and exemplary actions. Jesus has been understood in a variety of ways through the ages and his name, alone, is replete with meaning. The exercise of re-conceptualizing Jesus runs the serious risk of offending as well as the happy possibility of enlightening. With the goal of the latter in mind and respectful of the numerous ways of thinking about Jesus that have been used to understand him better throughout the centuries, I offer my own conception of Jesus, an idea that threads its way throughout the entire book, by characterizing him not as a prophet (in the tradition of Islam and Judaism), a great moral teacher (the Western intellectual tradition), a Messiah or Savior (Christian orthodoxy), but as a consumer and businessperson—a landlord, to be precise—and you, the reader, a person in search of consumer ideas, products, and services needed to create a meaningful and effective life.

Chapter One

Jesus Landlord

If Jesus was a carpenter, why didn't he build something?

Jesus has gotten an apartment ready just for us—single bed and bath with kitchen and a space to park our Hybrid. He has scrubbed the toilet, shampooed the rugs, dusted the shelves, sanitized the counters and sinks, and applied a coat of gleaming white paint to the walls—everything is ready to go for us. Jesus is just one among a host of landlords, leaders with smart ideas—corporate teams, politicians, money managers, scholars, entrepreneurs, artists, authors, speakers, designers, etc.—who offer to you and me rooms for rent. Jesus competes with these constituencies for our business. Let's try it—let's go ahead and sign an agreement with Jesus Landlord and see what happens. Now it is time to *live* in the apartment. We walk in and like most new renters we can hardly wait to make it our own—to turn *this place into our space*. We lay out some familiar dishware, set down a favorite chair and pillow, and fill the room with the sounds of our favorite singers and T.V. programs. What were once clean white walls are quickly filled with images, designs, and colors reflecting our experiences, memories, peculiar tastes, and preferences. As we take possession of our new apartment it undergoes a transformation and becomes barely recognizable from the one Jesus gave us the keys to just hours before. In our apartment, behind its closed door, we consume services, ideas and products in spaces available only to us and Jesus Landlord—unless we permit them, the world's landlords have no access to our apartment and its tiny consumer spaces. Does it bother them, knowing that millions of their constituents are out of sight, beyond their control? God only knows what goes on inside those apartments!

WHY ARE RELIGIOUS LANDLORDS SO CONCERNED ABOUT PLACES?

All landlords share a common purpose, which is to transfer increasingly more of their renters' personal power to themselves and the institutions they represent. In short, landlords seek ways to get renters to consume more of what they have to offer. Some landlords—both religious and otherwise—accomplish this by trying to convince Christians to do something Jesus taught against: to move out of the apartment God has generously provided them and into permanent real estate with lifetime contracts attached. For the thoughtful Christian, the tension boils down to this: Will he strike a deal with the landlords never stepping foot outside of their contracts and permanent *places*, or will he do business with Jesus and consume the world—with all its smelliness and evil, sweetness and compassion—in impermanent *spaces*. Here lies a central difference between your regular apartment and the apartment Jesus has in mind for us.

Unlike standard apartments, the apartments Jesus offers people are not defined primarily by their physicality and all that that implies. Dimension, size, cost, and layout—all the components dealing with the physical components of a building are of minor interest to Jesus. For him, buildings are spaces first and place second. Jesus taught and modeled the primacy of space over place. He may have been a carpenter in his early life, but in later life, Jesus is nothing of the sort. Rather, by the time of his ministry, his last months on earth, Jesus has become a designer, and he assumes the designer's perspective. In the final months of his life on earth, places have become important to Jesus *inasmuch* as they create living and vital spaces. Jesus is not a builder anymore, he has become an architect; he doesn't pick up the hammer, he oversees the construction. As a young adult in his village, Jesus voiced the concerns of the carpenter—the need to eliminate 1/4 instead of 1/8 off the door jam, the interest in using certain construction materials, and so forth. But during his ministry, we hear echoed in his teachings the sentiments and ideas of designers—Robert Venturi, Le Corbusier Peter Eisenman, I.M. Pei, Buckminster Fuller, and the great American architect, Frank Lloyd Wright, who said: "The space within becomes the reality of the building," "Space is the breath of art," and "Regard it as just as desirable to build a chicken house as to build a cathedral."

For Jesus, physical structures, whether they be cathedrals or chicken houses, don't just serve to protect their occupants against the outside elements or as loci for employment and commercial enterprise, but to provide settings for impermanent and permeable spaces where imagination and spiritual inventiveness are practiced. But we are getting ahead of ourselves. In order to understand Jesus' perspective on place and space, we first need to answer a fundamental question: "What is the difference between a place and a space?" First, place ...

Places are ordered according to proper rules and relationships. The bricks, sheet rock, and flooring of a place, such as a dentist's office, are situated beside each other, in coexistence, each in its own distinct location. Remove a window and the visual balance is disturbed. Knock out a beam and the structure is compromised. Places imply permanence, predictability, and stability. Because of its physicality, there is no room for give and take, for play. You are not permitted nor would you expect to walk into say, a U.S. Post Office building, knock a couple of bricks out of the wall and make a coffee table out of them, replace the blinds with curtains, tear out the yellowed linoleum and replace it with warm, golden oak slats, crank up your MP3, do the Funky Monkey with one of the mail clerks, make a prank phone call to the Postmaster General, and have some fun. Those kinds of activities happen in spaces. What is a space?

Spaces are composed of impermanent, movable components, independent of each other. Spaces may occur anywhere, including places. A city center with its fountains, buildings, shrubs, and grassy areas, is a planned place where pedestrians stop to talk, eat, read, make phone calls, flirt, day-dream, take in a few rays, and read the paper. City dwellers *consume* the city center. In so doing, they transform a place, carefully designed by city planners to exist for decades, into spaces that are here one minute and gone the next. These temporary spaces are the locations where Jesus expected his followers to practice his ideas, carry out his mission instructions, and consume goods, services, and experiences. The title of Jesus' new reality show isn't "Trading Places" but "Consuming Spaces." What is a space? De Certeau (1980) states it succinctly: "A space is a practiced place." Spaces filled with conversations and business negotiations, tinkling silverware, sloshing washing machines, screechy park swings, sidewalk performances, and hissing espresso machines—these are the "practice places" of Jesus' followers, the apartments offered by Jesus Landlord.

Why did Jesus prefer spaces to places?

> "The fox have holes and the birds have nests, but the Son of Man has nowhere to lay His head" (The Gospel of Matthew, 8:20).

Can you think of a single prominent landlord in the U.S. that does not have a place? The federal government has the White House and Capitol, the financial system has the New York Stock Exchange, corporations have their business centers, church denominations have their campuses and headquarters, and so forth. Landlords have always had places. You've got to have a place to work—right? But places serve as more than just a location to carry out the business of the organization. Within the sheet rock, glass and cement that make up a university campus, a church building, or corporate park, meaning "takes up residence." The material stands for something *im*material—for the dreams, ideals, values, and aspirations of the people who own it.

Why didn't Jesus create an organization, staff it, and locate it somewhere? Jesus was a carpenter. Why didn't he build something, for heaven's sake? These questions are worth contemplating as it is commonplace for a person aspiring to a level of influence to quickly secure a place for himself and members of his organization. The same is often true for the pastor of a new church.[1] Jesus didn't reject places completely; he understood that places have their place, that they even have the potential to advance his cause. He spent time talking with people in places—their synagogues, markets, homes, and businesses. Jesus respected places. He just didn't want to run his movement from one of them. Jesus was not interested in erecting a building which people could stand in front of—like the Microsoft headquarters, the Chicago Tribune building, Trump Tower, or a massive family estate—and say to themselves, "Now, that's power, that's influence, that's what Jesus is all about." Why?

Is the reason Jesus refused to build something was because it would be too materialistic of him to do so, too extravagant, too, well, "un-Jesus" to erect a humongous building and fill it with thousands of followers? No. Jesus wasn't afraid of material extravagance—he encouraged his followers to bathe his feet with expensive perfume (The Gospel of John 12). Nor was he categorically averse to material abundance—he filled his listeners with the hope of inheriting a future fit for a king, a life lived in mansions with countless rooms (The Gospel of John, 14:2). He didn't even seem to be particularly bothered by over-consumption—on at least one occasion he was criticized for being gluttonous (e.g., The Gospel of Matthew, 11:9).

Why Jesus preferred spaces to places is simple: places are too vulnerable, too open to attack and destruction. For the kinds of plans and ideas Jesus had for people, places simply weren't *powerful enough*. De Certeau (1984, p. 37) offers this simple but pithy observation: "Power is bound by its very visibility."

Americans are understandably uncomfortable admitting that the destruction of the World Trade Center on September 11, 2001 was both a material *and* immaterial spectacle. In the dust that rolled through the streets of lower Manhattan, one caught glimpses of something more than pulverized matter. In the Twin Towers resided ideals that were both reinforced and, as the events of 9/11 made painfully clear, left terribly vulnerable *by virtue of* the building's overwhelming material presence. This was the terrorists' principle goal: not the destruction of the material but of what it signified (i.e., the immaterial).

How extravagantly should Christians live, how many goods ought they to own, how big their bank accounts should be, and whether or not they should hold ambitions to make as much money as possible—to use an earlier example, all these are important *income* questions; all are incidental to the *consumption* question: "Place or Space?" Incidental because we know from the Introduction that there is a difference between income and consumption, that the size of our bank account may bear no relation to what's hanging in our closet. Income is just a number; consumption is a way of living. What this means is that, once we have decided for space above place, we can be as wealthy as Bill Gates and still consume faithfully, still be faithful to the Jesus' teachings.[2] In contrast, we can be a poor beggar, *but* if we insist on place over space, our fears and anxieties, our need to stay put and not risk it, our overriding desire to not change, manipulate, chew, consume—this will ultimately paralyze us, preventing us from doing our part in bringing about the full measure of Jesus' plan for people. How do we know when we have chosen well in our consumption choices? To know the man is to know his plan, so....

WHO WAS JESUS, WHERE DID HE GROW UP, WHAT WAS HIS OCCUPATION, AND WHAT WAS HIS SOCIAL STATUS?

Nathaniel said to him, "Can any good thing come out of Nazareth?" Philip said to him, "Come and see" (The Gospel of John, 1:46).

The story is told of Winston Churchill engaged in parliamentary debate with one of his political foes. Slowly but surely, Churchill destroys his opponent's argument. Reluctant to concede defeat, the man, exasperated, blurts out: "I don't care what you say, Mr. Churchill, I am entitled to my own opinions." To which Churchill replies, "Indeed, but you are not entitled to your own facts." It is difficult to separate fact from opinion when it comes to the person of Jesus, hard to separate Jesus, a Jewish peasant, from Christ, to whom Christians ascribe divinity. Who was Jesus, anyway? The list below helps us understand the man and his mission. This much we know for sure. Jesus was:

1. Poor (The Gospels of Luke 2: 24; 7:25; Matthew. 11:7-8)
2. Single (see Robinson (2005) "Jesus' Completely Unknown Sex Life, If Any," p. 96.
3. Perceived as illegitimately born (The Gospel of Mark 6:3)
4. An unconvincing voice and occasional embarrassment some members of his family (The Gospels of Mark 3: 21 and John 7:5)

5. Mentored by John the Baptist, but ultimately went his own way (see Robinson (2005), particularly chapter five: "Jesus was converted by John," pp. 111-139)
6. A first-century Jewish peasant (see Crossan's (1991) highly-acclaimed *The Historical Jesus: The Life of a Mediterranean Jewish Peasant.*)
7. A person who kept company with social outcasts (The Gospel of Mark 2:16)
8. Someone with a healthy appreciation for food and wine (The Gospel of Luke 7: 33-34)
9. A healer (The Gospel of John 9: 1-41)
10. An exorcist (The Gospel of Luke 8:26-39)
11. A person who fed hungry people (The Gospel of Mark 6:32-44)
12. An itinerant preacher (The Gospel of Matthew 8:19-20)
13. A monotheistic Jew who was intolerant of Roman polytheism (Goodman, 1987)
14. Penniless (The Gospel of Matthew 10:9-12)
15. Property-less (The Gospel of Matthew 8)
16. Defenseless (The Gospel of Matthew 10:9)[3]

Jesus was no "Josh Clean-cut." Were he to show up today, he would more likely be confused with Jack Kerouac or Mick Jagger than, say, James Dobson or your garden variety archbishop; the kind of guy airport security would undoubtedly ask to step aside. The list helps us to understand the person of Jesus. What characteristics, in particular, about Jesus help us understand his ideas about consumption?

The impact of occupation, social position, and locale on consumer behavior cannot be overstated. Where we spend the majority of our lives goes a long way in explaining how we consume and what we believe about consumption. I regularly ask my marketing students to identify several "consumer rules" their parents taught them. The most interesting differences revolve around financing: some of my students grew up in "plastic" families where everything from soup to cars was put on credit cards. Other students grew up in pay-as-you-go families. What's interesting is the impact of their parents' consumer behavior on their own. One student told me that the reason he was studying business was because he did not want to be like his father who had badly mismanaged the family's finances and had recently declared bankruptcy. (I learned later that his father was a heart surgeon.)

By just knowing something as simple as the size of the cities and towns that played a part in Jesus' world can provide invaluable insight into his consumer teachings and viewpoints. Here the most important towns and cities of Jesus' life appear in rank order, according to population:

- Rome—650,000 people

- Ephesus—200,000
- Antioch—150,000
- Corinth—100,000
- Jerusalem—80,000
- Damascus—45,000
- Capernaum—1,700

Oh, and one more place that figured prominently in the life of Jesus: his hometown, Nazareth. The town where Jesus spent the vast majority of his entire life consisted of approximately 125 souls! (Reed 1982)

Klinghoffer (2005, p. 44) writes: "The image persists of the typical Galilean as a hayseed."

Well, ouch. Dispensing with cultural stereotypes, research offers the best possibility of understanding the objective facts about daily life in the hamlet in which Jesus grew up. De Certeau's (1980) four-year study of a small French community uncovers ten characteristics that afford us insight into what life might have been like for Jesus in Nazareth. In tiny communities, De Certeau concludes:

1. Anonymity is impossible.
2. Vigilance is required as one cannot escape the possibility of meeting his neighbor nor can he be sure about what will be said.
3. Striking a balance between not getting too close to/not staying too far away from one's neighbors is an ongoing pursuit.
4. Knowing how to live with others is critical for personal happiness.
5. Learning to live so as not to be noticed or "to stand out" is important for successful living.
6. Social transparency is a core component (i.e., it is not only possible but important to know "who is doing what").
7. Proper behavior is measured against the backdrop of unspoken, tacit, and precise codes that specify what is acceptable language and behavior—something outsiders don't "get."
8. The body is the "blackboard" (particularly the face and hands) that display gestures and expressions that indicate whether or not the person is willing to adhere to the social contract of his small town.
9. There is a "gender-ized" organization to public space in the small community (e.g., the market is a space reserved for women; in certain bars only men are welcome).
10. Sex is not spoken about directly (i.e., one speaks "around" sex) but obliquely in allusions and innuendo that are often awkwardly crude or "dirty."

Of village life, Dobrowolski (1971) writes: Traditional culture manifests a tendency toward uniformity. It is expressed in the social pressure toward a common, unchanging pattern of social institutions and ideological contents within particular classes or village groups. *The individual, who deviates* from the commonly accepted pattern of behavior within his respective class or group, *meets with such repressive measures as ridicule, reproach, moral censure, ostracism, or even application of official legal sanctions.*

When our children were little, we often went to an Amish community not far from our Iowa home on Saturday mornings for fresh pastries, jams, and pies. It was easy to get lost in "Amish country" as the rural roads were not well-marked. About to leave a general store one Saturday, I asked one of the young Amish clerks, a teenager, how far it was to a nearby town. She replied, "I don't know. I have never been there." The town I had inquired was less than three miles away. I thought to myself: "Jesus in petticoats." Both Jesus and this young woman were products of tightly-knit, traditional, rustic, and isolated religious communities. Of course, there are differences between Jesus and this young Amish woman, three in particular:

First, we know that Jesus was an artisan peasant who likely made his living in the meager and undependable employment of affluent consumers. Americans think of peasants as simple country folk, accordion players who dance at the drop of a hat, and who lead pleasant and uncomplicated lives in bucolic settings. In Jesus' days, small town artisan peasants possessed three traits: 1) their survival was tied to city dwellers who desired the pots, baskets, and assorted products they handcrafted; 2) they were uneducated, most likely illiterate; and 3) their lives were by modern standards, miserable (Crossan 1998).

Second, on a social scale, we know that Jesus resided second-to-the-last, a single level above the "unclean and degraded class" of Roman society. He was a common laborer. "My boss is a Jewish carpenter," words proudly displayed on the bumpers of many a Bible Belt Buick, suggest an image of a robust worker, hammer in hand, confidently crawling atop scaffolding in a new subdivision. In truth, Jesus' low social standing was so stigmatized that the gospel writers hesitated to mention it, perceiving it as an embarrassment to his cause. Technically, Jesus was not a carpenter, but "the tekton" (Greek - Mark 6:3), which can be interpreted as carpenter, but is more likely indicative of a landless laborer.[4] Forget the image of Jesus with rolled sleeves and an impressive tool belt. Imagine instead a stooped migrant laborer, a share cropper squatting on the street corner hoping for work, accepting any wage offered. Seeing Jesus in their own time, some Americans would size him up as "an illegal" or condescendingly, a "wetback."[5]

Finally, we know that Jesus was, socially speaking, trapped. As a peasant, Jesus was not his own person and could never hope to be. As long as he stayed at his social position in life, his fate was tied to people who lived off his labor, who likely treated him despicably, and who lived their lives and spent their money far from the tiny social and commercial spheres in which Jesus and his friends and family resided. How did Jesus' rustic background impact his attitude to two of life's necessities?

WHAT WAS JESUS' ATTITUDE ABOUT HOUSING AND TRANSPORTATION?

"To walk is to lack a place." (De Certeau, 1984)

Jesus was an itinerant preacher and because of this, he was place-less—moving from place to place, space to space. Had he been *just* a person without a home, we would characterize him as a drifter, indigent, impoverished, homeless. But Jesus was on a mission; he was homeless and itinerant for a reason. Jesus walked from place to place with a purpose and, consequently, he created a "walking narrative"[6] that described what he believed was important and what was not. Jesus, like us, could walk anywhere he chose. Why did he choose one place and not another? This is an important question to ponder. In retrospect, we see that by going to some places and avoiding others, Jesus essentially made a selection that validated certain locations (the places he visited) and condemned others to inertia or disappearance (the places he avoided). The Sea of Galilee, Capernaum, an undisclosed mountaintop, certain back roads, a neighborhood water well, hidden walkways—these were some of the places Jesus chose to walk to and, consequently, turn into consumer practice-spaces. They are forever written in the annals of history. In contrast, the places he avoided, well known in his day—many of these have been lost to time.

Jesus' walking compositions are guided by codes (e.g., "love God with all your heart") that are informed by the Torah, Moses, and the prophets—codes that, as written earlier, he took seriously, albeit not necessarily literally. Referencing these codes and fueled by his own imagination, Jesus *moved beyond literal obedience required to be a good Jew to expressive interpretation*. He decides to go to the Sea instead of the Land in his walk one day in order to illustrate the point that in the midst of a dangerous storm, God can be depended upon. He walks to a wedding rather than the corner bodega on another day to compose a story of God's unexpected, eleventh hour generosity. Jesus doesn't *always* walk purposefully. The Pharisees and Jewish fundamentalists had a problem with this—they believed that if a person were truly faithful he would know exactly how God wanted him to consume, and therefore, he would stride purposely and without hesitation. Not Jesus. Sometimes he ambles along aimlessly; in the midst of murderous tension, he elects to "check out" and take a moment to scribble in the dirt (The Gospel of John 8:

1-11). His disciples expecting him any minute wonder, "where did he go this time" (The Gospel of John 6:22-27). Like the exceptionally skilled writer, he permits himself to drift, give his imagination room to play, perchance to stumble upon something he would have missed had he kept his walk to a set and strict routine. He consumes his day, his possessions, his relationships, his ideas, contemplating them, working them over. A good Jewish boy who was raised to unquestioningly follow the Jewish law to the letter, Jesus thinks better of it and tries a new approach.

Is this what Jesus had in mind for his followers, too? When he instructed them to go from village to village was he hoping to create a community of writer/drifters? If so, why; why move around? Why not just stay-put, settle down, create a *place*? Although Jesus does not condemn places, he knows that when people put down permanent stakes and refuse to drift, they run a risk of substituting their own consumer imagination with intractable beliefs framed by local legends, myths, and superstitions. Jesus had witnessed firsthand the effect when religious people refused to leave their insular communities, how their parochial village outlooks inclined them to put down immutable laws on how one ought to practice everyday life. He knew that there are lots of reasons to spend an entire lifetime in a single place, but that the desire for creativity, novelty, and change—these typically are not reasons why people stay put. Jesus is interested in creating and narrating new stories, not reinforcing old rumors—whether they be the rumors of a small village, a corporate culture, the national media, or a religious belief system.

WHAT KIND OF CONSUMER WAS JESUS?

The way Jesus lived, the things he taught, and his personal approach to space and place helps us identify a "consumer profile" consisting of ten essential characteristics. For the reader, they become points of comparison, standards by which to judge his own consumer behavior, and to ask: "Is this how I, too, am expected to live?" And addressed later: "Are there ways for me to express the principles Jesus propounded without literally following his actions and teachings?"

PROPERTY AND POSSESSIONS

1. *Jesus used, but didn't own.* Jesus occasionally used places owned by others to carry out his work as an itinerant preacher, but he did not own a place or secure a location to carry out his mission and live his daily life.[7]

2. *Jesus gathered with a purpose in mind.* Jesus appreciated material goods but showed no inclination to acquire and gather possessions for the sake of gathering (The Gospel of Matthew 6: 26).
3. *Jesus practiced a full social life; he was not a hermit.* Jesus ate, drank, and hung out. Although Jesus asked his followers to deny themselves, he did not specify the objects of which they should not deny themselves nor did he state in detail the literal consumer forms and patterns their personal denial should take (The Gospel of Mark 8: 34). Finally, Jesus did not practice severe asceticism, as did some of his contemporaries, most notably, John the Baptist (Matthew 9:14).[8]
4. *Jesus used material objects freely and eagerly; he was not an" anti-materialist."* Jesus used material possessions for specified purposes and was not against consumption, *per se* (The Gospel of Luke 24: 30). In fact, he was accused of being gluttonous and had a reputation as a person who enjoyed having a good time eating and drinking (The Gospel of Luke, 7: 33).

EMPLOYMENT

1. *Jesus maintained no steady employment.* Jesus did not have a job nor did he call his followers to particular vocations. Indeed, when Jesus called his disciples to follow him, he called them *away* from their livelihoods and into a life of itinerancy (Matthew 4:20).
2. *Jesus did not benefit materially from his skills and gifts; he operated pro bono.* Jesus exercised several spiritual gifts some of which, like healing, could have netted him a lucrative vocation, but he did not use any of his gifts or skills to benefit him or his group monetarily.
3. *Jesus did not seek employment to gain social acceptability.* Steady employment is a key not only to financial stability but acceptability before one's peers. Jesus showed no interest in this fact of life.

RELIGION AND CONSUMPTION

1. *Jesus advocated non-violence, non-resistance, and generosity; consequently, he did not defend or call on others to defend religious property and goods* (The Gospel of Matthew 5:44). Religion maintains a protective position to its properties and other material goods, and historically, religious groups have been willing to imprison and even kill those who threaten their material holdings. Jesus felt strongly about his Jewish homeland and its material presence, but he never advocated that it be defended against the Roman government nor did he advocate violence against those who had or would invade Israel.

2. *Jesus did not use buildings to establish the credibility of his new group.* New religious groups quickly acquire property to establish legitimacy in the eyes of others and success is frequently measured geometrically by the size of the group's holdings. Jesus' new group acquired no property and Jesus expressed no concern about this or the group's smallness.
3. *Jesus understood that material goods serve two functions: material and immaterial, and he did not confuse the material aspects of property with their potential symbolism.* Religious places provide more than a place to work and worship; they may also be used to symbolize traits important for the group's social acceptance, stability, and the perception of success. Jesus frequently used material goods as symbols (many examples follow), and he seemed to do so without mistaking a property's material components with its immaterial meaning.

IF WE WERE TO GIVE A NAME TO JESUS' APPROACH TO CONSUMPTION, WHAT WOULD IT BE?

Does Jesus expect us to live just as he did? Are we asked to literally apply his teachings about consumption to our practice of daily life? If so, the result of two millennia of Christian consumer behavior is a far-cry from the original plan. If we have not been called to literally apply but imaginatively consume Jesus' ideas and examples, how do we know when we have succeeded? We need a new name, a name for people who want to consume, relish the material gifts of the world, including the gifts of Jesus' life and teachings. Let's call it "Consumptianity," and let's define "Consumptianity" as: An approach to life designed to help people design apartments that Jesus, himself, would find comfortable enough to spend an evening in watching HGTV, browsing "Apartment Living" magazine, and munching on a bowl of organic Orville."

To faithfully practice "Consumptianity," are we required to take Jesus' consumer instructions literally? Next, we look at Christian groups that have attempted to do just that. How have they fared?

Chapter Two

Jesus Amish

What part of "own no property" don't we get?

After the Amish school shootings in October 2006 in which six school girls were killed, Americans expressed surprise and admiration for the Amish parents and friends of the victims as they quickly went to the side of the shooter's wife and family to offer comfort and reconciliation. One newscaster commented on their actions: "The message of Jesus is coming through loud and clear."[1] Having grown up around Old Order Mennonites, I have always known that the reason for their distinctive dress and lifestyle is directly connected to their faith; that their plain clothes, rejection of modern technology, and simple lifestyle are their attempts to take Jesus' consumer teachings literally; and that their commitment to the *Gemeinschaft*—the spiritual community characterized by common ownership, mutual care, and generosity—has nothing to do with socialism or any other political system, but that it's about Jesus' mission instructions and the example of early Christians.[2] Americans are apt to confuse the powerful teachings of Jesus exemplified in the Amish lifestyle with benign quaintness. For most Americans, Amish consumer lifestyles, their buggies and plain dress are associated with weekend outings.[3]

Who is responsible for this confusion? The onus for getting Jesus' message out and making sure it is correctly understood ultimately lies with Christians themselves, not those looking on. In this one terrible instance, the Amish way of interpreting Jesus' teachings was made clear for all to see. Normally, though, the Amish' suspicious attitude to modern culture and consumer goods along with their desire to distinguish themselves from nonbelievers, compels them to withdraw from society, frequently preventing them from helping outsiders understand the real reason they live as they do.

This explains why, ironically enough, it took a violent event to bring their commitment to nonviolence into the light of day. Without this sad event, the outstanding commitment of the Amish to Jesus' teachings exemplified in their lifestyles would have for many Americans continued indefinitely to be overshadowed by superfluities, like patchwork quilts and shoo-fly pie.

Does anyone beside the Amish take Jesus' consumer instructions literally? If so, who are these people and are they successful in their attempts to stay true to what Jesus asked? How does Consumptianity differ from traditional Christianity and its attitudes about consumption? We begin with a fundamental question: "Did Jesus ever issue a set of "consumption commandments?"

FIVE CONSUMER CODES THAT STOOD AT THE HEART OF JESUS' "MISSION INSTRUCTIONS"

Jesus did not articulate a set of "commandments" in the Old Testament sense of that word. He did, however, offer to those who would follow him five directives or codes about their consumption attitudes and habits, which are:

1. Unhesitatingly accept the generosity of others
2. Offer unbounded generosity in return
3. Hold no possessions
4. Hold no money
5. Carry no protection[4]

These five consumption directives are part of a group of teachings referred to as Jesus' "mission instructions." The first two principals have a nice, easy, "practice acts of random kindness" sound to them. They are not extremely easy to follow. On the other hand, it's awfully difficult to nail down if, when, and how someone actually practices or fails to practice unbounded generosity. What are we to make of the last three? These instructions, unlike the first two are extreme and unequivocal—either you are possession-less, penniless, and defenseless, or you're not. "Is Jesus *actually* asking us to divest ourselves of capital, property, and self-defense? Did Jesus expect us to take him seriously? Decide for yourself:

> Why do you call me: 'Master, Master,' and do not do what I say? Everyone hearing my sayings and acting on them is like a person who built one's house on bedrock; and the rain poured down and the flash floods came, and the winds blew and pounded that house, and it did not collapse, for it was founded on bedrock. And everyone who hears my saying and does not act on them is like a person who built one's house on the sand; and the rain poured down and the

flash floods came, and the winds blew and battered that house, and promptly it collapsed, and the fall was devastating. (The Gospel of Matthew, chapter 7)

The passage above is part of a group of teachings referred to as Jesus' "mission instructions." These verses constitute some of earliest recorded words of Jesus, suggesting that they are nothing less than Jesus' actual words. The gist of this teaching is simple: "Walk the walk." Jesus practiced what he preached by styling his life according to the five directives above, and that was what he expected of his followers. *Yes, Jesus really meant it!* In the earliest non-canonical source—(Q 10:5 – 6, 10 – 11)—and also in the Gospel of Luke: 9, Jesus' mission instructions include a description of the consumer lifestyle he had in mind for his followers: "Into whatever house you enter, first say: 'Peace to this house!' And if a son of peace be there, let your peace come upon him; but if not, let your peace return upon you .... Into whatever town you enter and they do not take you in, ongoing out from the town, shake off the dust from your feet."

In this passage, Jesus is not merely explaining proper etiquette. He is not saying: "This is how you, my followers, should act when you go to someone's house for dinner—be polite, but if your host is not very congenial, leave." It is more than this. Jesus was, in fact, prescribing that his followers adopt an itinerate lifestyle, like his own—that of journeying, unpaid preachers dependent on the generosity and hospitality of others. His mission instructions state: "You received without payment, give without payment" (Matthew 10:8) and "Carry no purse, nor knapsack, nor sandals, nor stick, and greet no one on the road" (The Gospel of Luke 10).

In short, the consumer lifestyle that Jesus followed and asked his disciples to follow was that of a *homeless, penniless, property-less, defenseless, non-compensated itinerant preacher who freely gives and receives material support*. Clearly, Jesus expected his followers to take his consumption commandments seriously. So, did they? The Amish notwithstanding, has any Christian group in the last 2,000 years strictly and literally followed Jesus consumer instructions? Some Christian leaders would reply that this question is irrelevant.[5] They believe that Jesus' consumer commandments were never meant to be followed by any but his immediate disciple group. Others believe that these consumption instructions are too impractical to carry out—we moderns can't be expected to follow them to the letter. They argue: "True, these instructions could be adhered to in Jesus' world—a simple, pre-consumer, Middle Eastern village—but how can we expect anyone to follow them in today's consumer society?"

Renowned biblical scholar, James M. Robinson is a proponent of this interpretation. He believes that Jesus' mission and the lifestyle of wandering poverty and defenselessness it prescribed was simply impractical within in a few short years after Jesus' death, by the time of Peter, Paul, Timothy, and other early church members. After all, Robinson argues, Jesus' ministry took him primarily to only three small Jewish villages in Galilee, all within walking or easy sailing distances of each other. In contrast, Robinson (2006) writes of a globe-trotting follower: "Paul did not hitch a ride on a sailboat to cross the Sea of Galilee (like Jesus), but must have bought a ticket ... on a ship to cross the Mediterranean."

The idea that Jesus' original teachings were not practical even for Paul is so evident to Robinson that he wonders why the writer of Luke even troubled himself with presenting what Robinson (2005, p. 146) refers to as Jesus' "antiquated Jewish mission" in the first place. He concludes: "Apparently Luke was treating these (early mission instructions of Jesus) more as a *museum piece* displaying how things had been done at the heroic beginnings." (Emphasis mine) Try telling that to a monk!

As impractical as Jesus' instruction and the consumer lifestyle he prescribed is to implement outside the tiny Galilean community in which he lived, the fact of the matter is that millions of Christians (and not a few nonbelievers) through the centuries have consciously and deliberately done precisely that—take Jesus at his word and follow his consumer instructions not only seriously, but literally. Jesus' severe mission instructions are still practiced by monastic Christians, missionaries, preachers, and just plain ordinary Christians and non-Christians—people who have the means available to live an affluent, independent life but reject it, choosing instead a life devoid of property, money, and protection. Who are these people?

WHAT IS "RADICAL CONSUMER CHRISTIANITY?"

When it comes to a literal reading of Jesus' mission instructions, the Amish are an exceptional case. Are there other models of faith that also take Jesus' consumer teachings literally? Yes, many, which we title here collectively *"radical consumer Christians,"* or simply, "radicals." Radicals are present in every Christian denomination, Protestant, Evangelical, Orthodox, Charismatic, and Catholic. Radical consumer Christians act sometimes as lone voices and sometimes with others in intentional faith communities, speaking to and carrying out the hard consumption teachings of Jesus in modern consumer society. They are people whose lives are clearly different from everyone else's. They consume differently, regularly fast and deprive themselves of material comforts and fat bank accounts in order to help the downtrodden and sick, unhesitatingly voice different often unpopular opinions about everything from war to fashion to Globalism, and they risk not only personal comfort and security but even, personal safety to enact Jesus' teachings. What do we know about radical consumer Christianity? What does it prescribe about consumption? Do we find within this category Christians who practice and have practiced all along what we are calling "Consumptianity?"

Although denominationally diverse, we can identify three historical "consumption assumptions" that are characteristic of many radical Christians and that provide the basis for their distinctive consumer behavior (Niebuhr 1957). First, many radicals believe that *culture is not "one, but two*": there is the world of nature (that is identified with Jesus' idea of "the Kingdom of the World"), from which faithful Christians keep their distance, and there is the world of spirit ("the Kingdom of God), to which they seek to draw near. For these Christina radicals, popular consumer culture—including the arts, fashion, entertainment, cultural movements, consumer styles, trends, and fads—are placed squarely in the Kingdom of the World and viewed with suspicion by most radical consumer Christians. After conducting a four-year investigation of conservative Christianity, *60 Minutes* producer, John Mark's, concludes in his book, *Reasons to Believe*, that for these believers, "The enemy... (is) the world," (2008, p. 111). For them, he continues: (The world) is an epithet, an imprecation ... a curse. It exists as a term of opprobrium that believers use for everything that tempts them away from God, evoking the very antithesis of holiness, the trap of this corrupted earth in which the devil, the flesh, and the desires of the heart endlessly festers.

Marks gives us a good picture of the radical stance on financial success and the consumer goods and experiences it yields, when he states:

> If you do especially well at sales in your business and take inordinate pride in that fact, you have begun to feel the creep of the world. If you buy an especially flashy car, build an especially big home, enjoy the company of especially beautiful and witty friends, you may be showing signs of having succumbed to the world (p. 112).

Second, many radicals embrace the consumption assumption that *goods are limited to their usefulness*—what goods "say" or symbolize (a principle aim of the fashion industry and modern marketing) is not important, possibly sinful. The Amish agree with this response, but, so do millions of Christians and non-Christians. The frivolous, extravagant, and excessive aspects of modern consumer culture along with its symbolism in the form of brands, logos, and ad slogans are judged by many as symptomatic of "what's wrong with our society." Millions of Americans, on principle, insist on owning nothing more than what helps them accomplish their daily tasks. They reject out-of-hand the products and services offered by large, multinational corporations and opt to buy and consumer locally.

Third, many radical Christian consumers adopt the consumption assumption that *culture is doomed*, a belief that branches in two directions, effectively forming two distinct Christian subgroups. One subgroup of radicals interprets the ultimate demise of culture as a reason to *withdraw* from it. These radical Christians often act as sideline, spectator critics of what they see as the whole pathetic outcome of a society that insists on adopting non-Christian and anti-Christian values. The second subgroup agrees with the first that culture is doomed but, unlike the first group, this belief *spurs them to action*, to jumping head first into society and all its problems. In the past, conservative Protestant groups were identified with the first subgroup while Mainline Protestant groups and Catholics were associated with the second.[6] What are the practical consequences of a worldview that sees culture as doomed? For the first subgroup, this belief leads members to separate from culture in order to lead lives focused on internal spiritual and personal transformation. For the second subgroup, it inspires a commitment to positive societal change, social outcry, activism, and the creation and practice of lifestyles and faith communities based, in part, on Jesus' consumption teachings. Different in their responses, both subgroups have at least one belief in common: that positive change in consumer society is limited, if not exceptional. Members of both subgroups often disagree on the details of what it means to live a faithful Christian lifestyle, but they have no disagreement on the bigger picture, the final destiny of a secular consumer culture—and it is not a pretty picture.

In summary, radical consumer Christians generally agree that while it is possible for one's possessions and consumer experiences to achieve positive outcomes, they also think that it is more likely that the bright side of consumption will be usurped by its dark side—materialism, greed, envy, anti-Christian values, and non-Christian lifestyles. Consequently, the radical attitude toward consumer culture is often judgmental and negative and many radicals in both subgroups often elect to create alternative expressions of consumer attitudes and behaviors—from home schooling to the creation of self-sustaining Christian communes to alternative holiday celebrations. History helps put the radical position into a clearer light.

WHERE DID RADICAL CONSUMER CHRISTIANITY BEGIN AND WHAT IS ITS HISTORY?

Not surprisingly, radical consumer Christianity has its roots in the teachings of Jesus, specifically, his mission instructions, the Sermon on the Mount, and the earliest writings of Jewish Christianity seen in the Q source and the Gospel of Mark.[7] Among the early church fathers, a spokesperson for the radical cause was Tertullian, who recommended that in order to be faithful believers should withdraw from "the bath, the inn, the weekly market, places of commerce, and from many occupations" (circa 207 A.D.). Tertullian follows Peter and Paul in offering specific and detailed instructions on what faithful Christians should and should not do. His instructions reach beyond daily consumption, but all his teachings conform to his interpretations of Jesus' and the Apostle's teachings.[8]

How did radical consumer Christianity wind its way through Christian history and through various Christian denominations, people, and traditions? Radical consumer Christianity surfaced indirectly in the *Protestant Church* in the sixteenth century in the so-called "counter-Reformation" led by Ulrich Zwingli, Conrad Grebel, and Menno Simons (George Fox, founder of the Quakers in the seventeenth century, is commonly placed in this tradition even though the society of Friends he founded originated some 100 years after the Reformation, and in England not Europe). Referred to variously as "Protestant sectarians," "Anabaptists," and "Radical Reformers," followers embraced a sharp division, identified earlier, between the Kingdom of the World and God's kingdom. The adoption of nonviolence and simple consumer lifestyles and an interest in using one's resources to help those in need stood at the heart of early Christianity. To this day, many sectarian groups are known particularly for their unwavering stands on nonviolence, simplicity, and service to victims of disaster, crime, and abuse. Their offspring encompass the *Mennonite* (from which the Amish originated), *Brethren, and Quaker* churches as well as conservative and non-liturgical churches that practice adult baptism, including some non-denominational, evangelical, and charismatic churches (discussed later).[9]

DID MARTIN LUTHER SUPPORT RADICAL CONSUMER CHRISTIANITY?

In a word, "no." The great reformer, Martin Luther, opposed radical sectarian ideas and even went so far as to endorse the imprisonment and killing (Corp. Ref. IV, 737 ff.) of some sectarian Protestants (later we will read why he felt so strongly).[10] This stance against sectarians, of course, is no longer held by Protestants. Indeed, some modern-day Protestants have adopted sectarian teachings (e.g., adult baptism and the division of church and state) and most hold sectarian groups in high regard because their unwavering commitment to and literal reading of Jesus' instructions. Exemplary is the twentieth-century Lutheran theologian, Dietrich Bonhoeffer. By any definition, Bonhoeffer was a radical consumer Christian who advocated literal obedience to Jesus' lifestyle teachings in small and intentional faith communities. His book, *The Cost of Discipleship*, spells out a literal interpretation of Jesus' consumer teachings for twentieth-century Christians and is a devotional classic. Today, many radicals—Protestant, Catholic, and sectarian—claim Bonhoeffer, who was an ordained Lutheran minister, as one of their own.[11]

CONSUMER RADICAL GROUPS IN THE UNITED STATES

Many recent American Christian sects are highly critical of culture, particularly consumer culture. Elements of radical consumer Christianity in the U.S. today are seen in the staunch rejection of culture by some *charismatic churches*, who find their roots in the American holiness movement (Pentecostal) of the early twentieth century, and whose best known spokesperson in the last century was Oral Roberts, the founder of a university and hospital devoted to spiritual and physical healing. Representatives of this group also include the *Vineyard Ministry*—a national organization that includes 1,500 churches worldwide—who, like other charismatic communities, practice speaking in tongues in their worship services.[12] Charismatic Christians are loosely organized and rarely act in concert on the public stage, preferring rather to retreat to communal and private religious experiences and the exercise of spiritual gifts. While many charismatic Christians advocate the rejection of a variety of aspects of culture, personal spiritualism guides and takes precedence over most expressions of consumer behavior.

Another popular and fast-growing group in the U.S., *Evangelical Christianity*, originated in the nineteenth-century British revival movements, and more recently, in the Billy Graham Crusades of the middle twentieth century. Many Evangelicals oppose select aspects of culture and they have become politically outspoken against U.S. consumer culture, especially since the election of Ronald Reagan to the U.S. Presidency in 1980 (Wilentz, 2008). Evangelicals delineate sharply between the kingdoms of God and the world. However, while Evangelicals are apt to reject consumer culture, especially its "pop culture" expressions, they are not as likely to embrace everyday habits of simple living, intentional poverty, nonviolence, nonresistance, and commitment to the poor. An exception is seen in the so-called "radical evangelical movement." Started in the 1970's by journalist and Christian peace activist, Jim Wallis, radical evangelicals initially attracted disenchanted 1960's religious civil rights and peace advocates as well as a radicalized portion of the so-called "Jesus People" movement of the 1970s. *Sojourner Magazine*, which Wallis created, advocates non-violent resistance and simple lifestyles based on the teachings of Jesus and lived-out in small faith communities. Jim Wallis is not a household name to most American Christians and except for an occasional appearance on T.V. talk shows, he has never assumed the high profile of religious crusaders like Graham or Roberts. Nevertheless, his book, *Gods' Politics: Why the Right Gets it Wrong and the Left Doesn't Get It* (2005), was a best seller.

Finally, *Fundamentalist Christians* have traditionally been radically exclusivist, prescribing strict rules and beliefs for "true Christians." Fundamentalism rose to national prominence in the 1920s during the so-called "Scopes Trial," which debated the teaching of evolution in public schools, and until recently its most prominent spokesperson was the late Reverend Jerry Falwell. Fundamentalists have joined with many Evangelicals in selectively criticizing specific cultural expressions—Hollywood, the gay community, liberal politics, same-sex marriage, and abortion rights, while largely ignoring others, such as poverty, environmentalism, economic injustice, and war and peace.[13]

HOW DO CATHOLIC AND PROTESTANT CONSUMER RADICALS DIFFER?

Radical consumer Christianity is most evident in the *Roman Catholic Church* in the lives of those designated by the Church as saints. One of the better known saints, Francis of Assisi, rejected the lofty social position into which he was born for the life of a religious ascetic in his attempt to take Jesus' teachings literally. Today, radical consumer Christianity is most evident (but not exclusively so) in the lives of "the Religious" (nuns, priests, and monks), many of whom have taken vows of material poverty.[14] Catholic radicals, such as Dorothy Day who founded the Catholic Worker Movement and who have never taken the vows of the Religious, include countless and unknown believers.

Why distinguish between Catholic and Protestant consumer radicals? There is one significant difference between Protestant and Catholic radicals and that is, for Catholic radicals, pessimism about culture and man-made institutions is not total, as with many Protestant radicals. In particular, for Evangelicals and charismatic Christians, the tension between Jesus and culture is fundamental and sets a mostly negative tone and prohibitive direction for Christian conduct, including consumer behavior. In contrast, Catholic radicals, in accordance with Catholic orthodox teachings, believe that all creation and culture, including consumer culture, has been and is being redeemed by Jesus' death and resurrection, and that it is their personal responsibility to enact that redemption by being "the face of Christ" in society.[15] Following Pope John Paul's II analogy, reconciliation, like Jesus' robe, "is seamless," extending from the poorest of the poor to the richest of the rich, from the homeless shelter to palaces, from the womb to the battlefield to the execution chamber. In short, Catholic faith teaches followers to be active in and hopeful about the world—all of it. How does this attitude play out in the Catholic's daily life? Traditionally, Catholics have been less prone to consumer prohibitions than their conservative Protestant counterparts, participating, for example, in legalized gambling and imbibing in tobacco and alcohol products, none of which have been officially condemned by the Catholic Church[16] (A dear friend, a cradle Catholic, maintains that the best priests are those who love their Scotch and can appreciate a good cigar—characteristics that would condemn many conservative Protestant pastors to certain unemployment). This is not to say that Catholic radicals don't judge many consumption practices and habits to be sinful. They do. But, unlike their Protestant counterparts, they do not categorically judge consumer culture and its artifacts as hopelessly doomed. The Catholic radical's hope-filled view of material goods, property, and money is seen in a common Catholic affirmation: "All is gift." Protestant theologian, H.R. Neibuhr (1951), summarizes the position of the Catholic Church and its radical members when he writes that they "cannot separate the works of culture from the grace of God. But neither can they separate the experience of grace from cultural activity."

NON-CHRISTIAN, ANTI-CONSUMPTION MOVEMENTS IN THE U.S.

My wife and I regularly visit southern California where we enjoy spending time on the beaches. With our van as home, we meet many people, including homeless individuals. We have found that a number of homeless people, who claim no religious affiliation, are homeless *on principle*. A sizeable portion of the homeless people we have met in our California travels live simple lives without a permanent home or the trappings of modern life not just because they want to live this way but because they believe it is the right thing to do. One such person, Jim, has been living for forty years with his V.W. bus as home. For six months he lives in California, working when he needs money, but otherwise, enjoying ocean swimming, tennis, and beach life. When winter arrives in southern California, he heads for Indonesia where he spends time in remote areas helping develop schools and working with impoverished people. My wife met another person, Anne, while enjoying a three dollar shower at a beach bathhouse. Anne has lived in the back of her Toyota pickup for twenty years. Her main concern in life is that she "leaves no carbon footprint." A vegetarian, she leads a simple life that requires little electricity or fuel of any kind.

Radical consumer ideology (as opposed to theology) is not just for Christians or confined to a few eccentrics. It has been advocated by several, highly influential *non-religious groups and spokespersons*. Historically, these groups have their roots in Western anti-consumerism movements which can be traced to the early eighteenth-century. (Outright social/political protests against consumerism were rare before the twentieth-century). In earlier times, views of consumption and overindulgence in the U.S. were often linked and associated with sickness, the ways of the city, and the downfall of society. Both Kellogg (of boxed cereal fame) and Graham (creator of the Graham cracker) were nineteenth-century proponents of vegetarianism, and both were outspoken critics of over-consumption, which they linked to moral depravity. In the early part of the twentieth-century, consumerism was viewed by anti-consumption groups as promoting "uppity" behavior and seen as a threat to traditional morality. Children's literature in the U.S. encouraged kids to reject highfalutin consumer lifestyles and be resigned to their lot in life (Stearns 2001).

Are Jesus' consumer teachings and secular anti-consumption beliefs one and the same? If they are (and they aren't) they surely haven't gotten the results Jesus envisioned. From early on, some secular anti-consumption groups have used their beliefs vindictively to attack particular groups. Targeted groups included: *women* (whose shopping was perceived to be the result of their inherent moral weakness, irrationality, flightiness, and frivolousness) (De Grazia and Furlough 1996), *Jews* (whose ownership of large American department stores were viewed as evidence of their desire to grow wealthy and exercise inordinate influence over society), *foreigners and foreign culture* (particularly the French who were integrally involved in Western fashion trends and trade), *homosexuals* (as consumerism was linked to effeminacy and "softness"), and *African Americans* (because of their "flashy clothing," evidenced in race riots in the 1940s against "zoot-suited Negroes") (Stearns 2001). Of course, these attitudes were not limited to nonbelievers but have been shared over the years by many Christians too. Finally, twentieth-century groups that adopted anti-consumerism positions have run the political gamut, from the Nazis (De Grazia, 1981), who advocated traditional German consumer culture (dress, values, foods, etc.) to the Socialists, whose anti-consumerism originated in their anti-capitalism.[17] Anti-consumerism has long been associated with European and American intellectualism, and twentieth-century anti-consumerism targets have included Christmas commercialism, so-called "sin products" (most notably tobacco and alcohol products), and the U.S. film and media industry.[18]

Along with food and dress, health and fitness has been a favorite anti-consumption target. In the early 1900's, "posture training schools" sprang up in response to the softness of Americans brought on by their growing reliance on the conveniences and comforts of consumer products. The posture movement faded with World War II, but its moral overtones continued in dieting and weight loss movements beginning in the 1970s which helped to spawn a billion dollar industry of tapes, books, foods, sports and fitness equipment, clothing, magazines, catalogs, and wellness centers (Stearns, 1997). Today, dieting and physical fitness signify strength of character in an American society populated by over-indulgent consumers, and verbal attacks on overweight people and people who neglect to exercise frequently often take on the characteristics of a moral crusade according to the extensive research on weight loss support groups conducted by Natalie Allon. (Sadly, Dr. Allon was severely disabled in a car accident before much of her research was published in refereed academic journals and no published references are available. She died in 2001. I have acquired and read most of the little-known and rigorous research conducted by Dr. Allon.) Finally, the anti-smoking campaigns that began in the 1970's (which sprang from both religious, moral and recently, medical concerns) mirrors the alcohol abstinence and temperance movements of the 1920's with the banning of smoking in private and public areas and the regulation of cigarette advertising beginning in the 1970s. Unlike the weight loss movement, the anti-smoking movement began early in the American twentieth-century with Fundamentalist Christianity, but recently, religious overtones have been overshadowed by medical findings on the harmful effects of smoking on one's health and today, anti-smoking "sermons" may be completely devoid of religious import.

Anti-consumerism is seen in media programs and spokespeople who advocate extreme left- and right-wing political positions with moral and sometimes, Christian overtones. In both Christian and secular radio and television talk shows, radical consumer Christian and secular anti-consumption viewpoints are frequently expressed in oppositional and antagonistic manners. Although few media representatives engage directly in political activism, they cannot they be described as removed from the cause as they command large media audiences for who they serve as vital sources of information. Magazines, news/entertainment show hosts, radio and T.V hosts, even certain cable T.V. networks, such as Fox News, MSNBC, PTL (conservative Christian television), EWTN (Catholic television channel), and Comedy Central, daily and nightly parade anti-consumption social/political positions—from environmentalism to economic injustice to materialism—to audiences who number in the tens of millions. Finally, in recent U.S. history, politically active and outspoken anti-consumerism groups have included the Hippies (Perry, 2005), Yippies (Rubin, 1970), and recently, Ad Busters (since 1989), a not-for-profit, anti-consumerism organization that publishes a magazine (of the same name) that advocates activism against mass media by producing commentary on itself—so-called "culture jamming" (Heath and Potter, 2004). The most popular culture jamming programs on television are *The Daily Show* with John Stewart and *The Colbert Report,* both commanding nightly audiences of 10 million viewers-plus, and both of which adopt a culture-jamming format that originated in the 1970s with the Saturday Night Live television program newscasts (Lasn, 2000).

We conclude by addressing an earlier question: "Are radical Christianity and Consumptianity one and the same?" It would be a mistake to confuse Consumptianity with radical consumer Christianity or secular anti-consumerism. How do they differ? The most important difference lies in the radical's view of how goods "ought" to be used. For radicals, the *use* of goods is measured, conservative, and pragmatic—things are valued primarily as means to ends, and the *expressive* role of goods—what objects mean or have the potential to mean—is often ignored or denigrated by anti-consumption groups, even viewed by some conservative Christian groups as sinful. Similarly, material extravagance is seen as having little or no potential to effect good. In the next chapter, I explain why this purely utilitarian perspective sharply contrasts with Jesus' own teachings and behavior. I make the case for a positive Christian consumerism, arguing that with material goods and experiences, Jesus seized the opportunity to make people's lives better. I explain how material goods hold the potential to enhance the Christian's imaginative play and embolden his intent to follow Jesus.

Chapter Three

Jesus Contractor

Are some cars more Christian than others?

While a college student in the early 1970s, I attended an evening workshop designed to help students understand the beliefs of a Christian group who, in retrospect, I now know clearly fell in the radical consumer Christian category. The speaker, a church leader, suggested that driving certain cars was more faithful to Jesus' teachings than driving others. He even named names: inexpensive cars like Volkswagens (this was the 1970s), he maintained, are an example of "good Christian cars" whereas expensive cars, like Cadillacs, aren't. The man's suggestion shows us how Christians use material objects to express faithfulness, or lack thereof. This has been true since the Church's beginnings. When Jesus died, he essentially contracted out his mission to those left behind. How'd that turn out?

NEW TESTAMENT (POST-JESUS) CONSUMER TEACHINGS

One way followers of new movements gain acceptability after their leader has died is to use material objects—clothes, houses, consumer articles—as receptacles for meaning. The letters written by the apostles to the early churches are replete with ideas on how being followers of Jesus should impact their practice of daily living, their consumer habits and lifestyles. One example of this is seen in Peter's instructions to Christian women.[1] He instructs them against "plaiting the hair, and of wearing of gold, or of putting on of apparel" (I Peter 3). Why did Peter feel this way? It is because in his day, these specific articles and styles were commonly used by the wealthiest citizens and also prostitutes. For a new religious movement hoping to attract a following, Peter understandably did not want non-believers to draw the wrong conclusion about its followers. Since only a small portion of Christian women still take Peter's and many of the other apostles' instructions literally, what relevance do Peter's teachings, and many New Testament teachings, have for modern consumer Christians?

What is interesting about Peter's instruction for us moderns is not the instruction, *per se*, but what it implies, namely, a keen awareness on Peter's part about the symbolic power of goods. Simply put, Peter is not concerned about the particular items of gold and styles of hair themselves, but about what the wearing of certain items *says* to non-believers. Using our earlier terms, Peter is focused on the space-ness of the material good—the consumption experience—not the place-ness of the material good, the actual physical components (i.e., physicality) of the objects themselves. (The struggle to understand the differences between what Peter said and what he meant is not unique to him or any other early Christian spokespersons. Cultural signification invariably becomes muddled over time, especially when that which is being signified is instruction, religious instruction no less, that originated in well-defined and colloquial cultural contexts but has over time "gone global," as was the case with Peter's instruction.)

Today, ideal Christian faithfulness is still evidenced when Christians wear or refuse to wear certain styles of clothes or don particular symbols. Like Peter, many Christians understand that their material possessions consist of more than the physical components of cloth, metal, jewels, and wood. Within the components of their possessions resides meaning that connotes something about their own closely-held principles of faith. The purchase by a church pastor of an expensive German luxury sedan, for example, may signal to people in and outside the church that extravagant spending does not violate Jesus' teachings. In contrast, a pastor who encourages parishioners to purchase "fair trade" food, used clothing, and furniture made by entrepreneurs in less developed countries probably signals a very different message about faithful Christian consumer behavior.

We'll never know whether or not Peter would feel the same way today about jewelry, hair style, and adornment, defending before modern Christians his earlier instruction to the letter. It's probably the case, as we read shortly, that while Peter certainly intended for his instructions to be taken literally at the time he wrote them, he did not deliver these consumption directives as Christian "consumer commandments" to be taken literally by all Christians for all times. Ironically, those who insist on a literal reading may be violating the very spirit of Peter's instruction (and, as we read shortly, Jesus' intentions too). Ironically, the literalist shows a willingness to do with Peter's instructions what, in the long term, Peter probably would not have advised. But how can we be so certain that Jesus and the early Christian writers did not expect future followers to apply their consumption rules literally, word-for-word?

Are humans "literal" beings?

Micro-observations of human behavior by cognitive psychologists offer this interesting insight: Humans are anything but literal beings.[2] They do not remember most things literally; they do not receive much less follow most instruction literally. Instead, they interpret and infer; they make it up as they go along. Most of our behavior is constructed on sight, in the moment, with the material that we have immediately at hand. The human mind is not a passive blank slate but an active "re-constructor" of visual and verbal information. Even the minimum-wage worker who is asked to follow the same instructions day after day injects his own interpretation and personal expression into his work. In her award-winning book, *Nickel and Dimed* (2005), *New York Times* journalist, Barbara Ehrenreich, records the events of a year spent undercover as a low-wage employee. Rather than mindlessly and passively adhering to their employers' instruction, Ehrenreich found that many workers tailored their supervisors' instructions, injecting their own individual interpretations, and that this expressive license was an important aspect of getting through a day of, otherwise, tedious and meaningless work. Along with the person who owns his own company or the executive who enjoys a million dollar salary, the wage earner *consumes* his employment too. He alters the rules set down and makes attempts to bring novelty and imagination to the tasks assigned. Why? Is it because he is a rabble-rouser, a hooligan, a trouble-maker? No, it is because he is a human being, "programmed" to actively consumes the things and experiences he encounters hour-by-hour, moment-by-moment.

Ehrenreich's observations of minimum-wage workers in America concur with De Certeau's who described the French consumers he studied for four years as immigrants, wanderers, aliens (interesting that these same titles are commonly applied to God's followers in both the Old and New Testament) who seize moments in their day as opportunities to exercise power over the strong, such as their employers, law enforcement, their family, and government officials. De Certeau records that these consumers' ways of operating include clever tactics which help them "get away with things"—maneuvers, discoveries, and tricks that permit them to exercise temporary power, albeit meager, over the strong.

Was Jesus any different? If not, what were the tricks and maneuvers he used to "get away with things," to exercise power over the authorities? We gain insight into what Jesus thought of change and the methods he prescribed for its achievement, when he states:

> And no one puts new wine into old wineskins; otherwise the new wine will burst the skins and will be spilled, and the skins will be destroyed. But new wine must be put into fresh wineskins. (The Gospel of Luke 5: 37-38)

In his use of common consumer objects (i.e., wine and wine containers) to symbolize and express his deepest-held beliefs, we see Jesus employing pedagogy, his principle mode of educating others. The same is true for us. As we use consumer objects to conduct our daily lives, we also *invariably* use these possessions to build immaterial expressions. In other words, we, like Jesus, use our possessions to construct meaning—but how? How do we use our possessions to construct meaning and effect change? According to business and social researchers, there are two possible ways to carry this out: First, by using parts of the old system (the way things have long been done) we reformulate an old idea into a new one and second, by using new objects we construct completely novel meaning—meaning that mirrors our personally held beliefs and ideals (McCracken 1988). For example, when Christians take ancient worship practices and incorporate into them rap music and urban graffiti they construct meaning, much like Jesus who used traditional Jewish consumer staples, bread and wine, to speak in a fresh way about God's saving love for humanity. When churches use a Web-based marketing model to enhance their ministries, they construct meaning by introducing new ideas incomprehensible to Christians a generation before them, again, like Jesus who by talking with tax collectors, women, and other "undesirables," exemplified notions about the family of God that were extremely difficult for his contemporaries to fathom.

Jesus unabashedly and wholeheartedly used concrete, material objects in wholes and parts to construct new principles and reframe old ones. His approach to the material world stood in sharp contrast to the ways of his Jewish counterparts (and many radical consumer Christian groups today) who, instead of showing how people might use material objects to construct and express meaning, were more interested in showing people how to live according to onerous prescriptions and punitive laws governing the use of goods. One may counter: "But the traditional use of goods has worked for centuries. It worked for the Jews of Jesus' day and it continues to work for radical consumer Christian groups, like the Amish and other conservative Christians. Why question it?" It is true that, to an extent, a literal approach to religious instruction works and we have millions of examples and centuries of practice as evidence. But this approach works best, if at all, only under certain conditions; namely, a literal rendering of Jesus' and the apostles' instructions succeeds in *places removed from the spaces* where most of the world's inhabitants live and consume. As long as they stayed in their insular, isolated communities, all was well with the Jewish people of Jesus' day. The problems began when people—like Jesus, John the Baptist, and the prophets—pushed them to move out of familiar places into strange and unfamiliar spaces, to leave their homes and walk about, to focus their attention on the consumption of their objects not the objects themselves, to think about God and God's family in new ways, to drift and to open themselves to the world outside their safe, quaint, and slightly quirky communities. For Jesus and his followers, life and faith may be comparatively smooth *as long as* it is conducted in places disconnected and disengaged from the Kingdom of the World.

WHY LITERAL ISN'T GOOD ENOUGH

Then Pharisees and scribes came to Jesus from Jerusalem and said, "Why do your disciples break the tradition of the elders? They do not wash (their) hands when they eat a meal." He said to them in reply, "And why do you break the commandment of God for the sake of your tradition?"

He summoned the crowd and said to them, "Hear and understand. It is not what enters one's mouth that defiles that person; but what comes out of the mouth is what defiles one." Then his disciples approached and said to him, "Do you know that the Pharisees took offense when they heard what you said? (The Gospel of Matthew 15: 1-3, 11-12)

Jesus' instruction is still offensive, sometimes nudging and sometimes kicking us into the Kingdom of the World, compelling us to change it and bring the Kingdom of God to life. One way this happens is through the construction of new meaning in our material possessions. For us, those who practice Consumptianity, we have no interest or intention in taking Jesus' or Peter's consumption instructions literally. That would be inefficacious, lame. For us, it is about the expression of his principles in our daily consumption. For us, it is not, how in the world do I relinquish all my money and property in order to be faithful to Jesus' teachings, but how do I *express* homelessness, even while living in an affluent suburb; how do I *express* abject poverty, even while earning a six-figure salary? This may sound like a cop-out, but it is just the opposite. I assert and eventually explain that there is potentially as much if not more power to change the world in the expression of poverty as in its actual accomplishment—and Jesus is our best example of this very thing. How so?

When Jesus constructed new meaning, refusing to adhere to the old system of religious rules, the impact on the religious and political "old boys," the primary landlords of his day, was immediate and the outcome was impressive—a simple, country peasant and twelve followers managed in the course of months to shape the ancient and, eventually, Western world without traveling to more than a half a dozen towns within a fifty mile radius of their homes. Jesus could never have had such an effect had he been a Messiah like Klinghoffer envisions, had he insisted on a literal following of Jewish rules and expectations carried out in small religious communities, had he been, merely, a "really good Jew." What makes us believe that the only way to significantly change our lives, our families, and our world, is to be "really good Christians?"

"RAT-CAT-DOG" MAN

Could only a person like Jesus have pulled something like this off? Does only a person like Jesus have the imagination to use objects expressively to change people's lives for the better, to conduct an enormously impressive religious life even while consciously refusing to literally apply centuries-old religious rules? Over the last few years my wife and I have become acquainted with a homeless man who travels about with three animals in tow: a dog, a cat, and a rat. A college educated person, he has trained these three natural enemies to coexist peacefully. His message is simple: if these three animals can learn to live with each other, then why can't we humans do likewise? Walking down the street, passersby marvel at the scene, observing the cat carefully grooming the rat and the dog affectionately playing with the cat. It wasn't long before the odd quartet showed up on You-Tube. Last I looked, the video had registered over two million hits! Today, it is difficult to have a quiet conversation with the "rat-cat-dog man," as hundreds of people, mostly tourists, snap pictures of him and his tiny team of peacemakers.[3] We have noticed that those waiting in line to snap a picture often have a pensive look as they are given time to reflect on the meaning of the scene. Watching their faces, my wife and I observe surprise and delight slowly turn to thoughtful "what-if" reflection.

Like this gentleman, like Jesus, people have always had at their disposal the material goods required to thoughtfully alter their world. This is particularly true in today's hi-tech world. As recently as the 2008 U.S. elections, we saw how a well-timed "You-Tube" entry composed on a $500 computer in someone's basement brought a national leader, a potential presidential candidate, to his knees. Jesus' parables are not greatly different from a live Web cast or "blog." For Christians, their clothing, houses, and church buildings have always acted (whether they like it or not) as "offline blogs"—bulletin boards where messages are posted, from personal opinion and debate to dissatisfaction, alternative viewpoints, values, and ideas. Like a pithy parable or a well-timed cyber blog, things happen when Christians use their material goods to express deeply-held beliefs: their possessions stimulate in-group dialogue and they inform others outside the group about their personal beliefs and principles.

Consumptianity asserts that the potential for the expressive power of goods far surpasses the impact of a literal following of rules about their usage. This week thousands of churches will meet to consider the message of reconciliation that Jesus preached, but how many will change their lives and others' lives as a result of their strict obedience to Jesus' teachings? On the other hand, the message of hope reaches hundreds each hour, every day thanks to the thoughtful and imaginative work of a single homeless man who has decided to utilize the few things he possesses to express a timeless message. We would be remiss to not utilize this power to tell people what we believe. But how do we accomplish this?

RUBBER BABY BUGGY BUMPERS

One of our sons attends college in Santa Barbara. My wife and I really enjoy visiting him there but he has become suspicious that the reason we visit so often has less to do with him and more to do with the sunny weather and beaches. Because of its wonderful weather and lovely beaches, Santa Barbara is an expensive place to live. The average income there is approximately $100,000 and in the neighboring community, the *average* income stands at a staggering $250,000 a year. Knowing this, I still wasn't prepared for the $2,500 price tag on a baby buggy in a store window on State Street in Santa Barbara's main commercial center. How does a product that can be easily purchased for less than $50 command such a price? There has to be more going on here than simply transporting little Johnnie through the neighborhood. Fifty million dollar homes and sports cars worth hundreds of thousands of dollars—why are consumers willing to pay prices that far exceed the product's function? Contrastingly, how does a wristwatch worn by one's father and worth less than $20 become a possession the owner is not willing to sell, no matter how much he is offered (Belk, Wallendorf, and Sherry 1989)? The answer lies in the *meaning* our products possess. How is product meaning constructed? Researchers tell us that the process follows six steps, seen below.[4] The material in the table is pretty complicated, so I quickly follow with an example using an ordinary consumer product: (you guessed it) a baby buggy.

INSTRUMENTAL MEANING

1. *Categories*. Cultural categories (age status, class, gender, religious membership, political affiliations, career, etc.) organize our world.
2. *Principles*. Cultural principles organize our ideas.
3. *Activities of Everyday Life*. The expression of cultural principles takes place in the activities of our daily living.

EXPRESSIVE MEANING

1. *Goods*. Goods express the principle.
2. *Cultural Principles to Goods*. Education moves the meaning of the principle from culture (where it exists as an abstract, material-free idea) to the good (where it exists symbolically, as a sign pointing to the idea).
3. *Goods to Consumers*. Rituals move the meaning of the principle from the product to the person who consumes it. Consumer rituals include: a. *"possession rituals"* (the act of personalizing the product); b. *"grooming rituals"* (the preparations made for "going out" with the product into the public); c. *"exchange rituals"* (in the case of gift giving, where the giver invites the recipient to define himself in his (the giver's) terms; and d. *"divestment rituals"* which involves disposing of the product, such as throwing it away or giving it to another person when one is finished using it.

Consulting the above and interfacing its information with what we know about the role and function of a baby carrier, we understand that cultural categories in this instance are derived from our understanding of human development, which may be categorized as: infancy, toddler-hood, elementary-aged children, junior-high children, high-schoolers, young adults, adults, middle-age adults, older adults, old and dependent adults. The category in this instance is "Toddler-hood" (see 1 above). The cultural principle may be stated as: "The safe and responsible transportation of toddlers depends on the assistance and care of willing and capable adults" (see 2). The expression of this principle is observed in the everyday activity of safely and responsibly transporting young toddlers in their community (see 3).

Up this point, people who hold strong anti-consumption attitudes and beliefs, like many radical consumer Christians, have no problem with the role played by their possessions. According to Steps 1-3, products are purely utilitarian, meant to get a job done, to get little Johnnie around town—period. But there's more ...

The baby carrier materially expresses the *immaterial cultural principle* of the safe and responsible transportation of young children (see 4 above). Using formal and informal sources (e.g., other young parents, the media, advertisements, salespeople, credentialed experts, family members, etc.) to educate themselves about baby carriers, *the meaning of the principle is moved to the good* as the parent decides what kind of carrier to purchase, such as: a trendy carrier, the safest carrier, the most expensive carrier, the least expensive carrier, a used carrier, a carrier with special meaning that is passed down from a family member, etc. (see 5). Rituals *move the meaning of the principle from the baby carrier to the parent* (i.e., the consumer) who, using it to transport his child in the community, is perceived by those in his community in a particular way (positively or negatively, responsible or irresponsible, indulgent or a penny-pincher, middle-class or upper-class, etc.) because of the meaning that resides in the carrier he is seen using to transport his child (see 6).

To summarize, Steps 1-3 tie goods to culture in a literal and pragmatic way. In the activities of our daily lives—making coffee in the morning for our spouse, attending meetings at work, and taking our child to his piano lessons—*we accomplish* our everyday routines and rituals with the assistance of cultural categories and principles that act as organizing structures and codes. Steps 4-6 tie goods to culture in a *non*-literal and expressive way. In the making of our morning coffee *we communicate* a steadiness and dependability to ourselves and our spouse; in our attendance at meetings we show respect for our colleagues and enthusiasm for our work; in taking our child to piano lessons we show parental conscientiousness and optimism for our child's potential to learn. To use an earlier example, if we were to stop at Step 3, we (those who are believers) would have no recourse but to follow Peter's instructions about hair and adornment to the letter. Moving beyond, we are given creative freedom to use current hair and clothing styles, as did Peter in his time and culture to say something about our most deeply-held principles. There is yet one more quality to the six steps....

All six steps, researchers have found, are *inevitable*. The inevitable quality of meaning construction is important to ponder. Those who hold strong anti-consumption beliefs are apt to deny that they are affected by their possessions ("my clothes say nothing about who I really am; I do not buy one pair of shoes over another for comfort only, not because I want to express myself"). Or consumer radicals may negatively judge people, such as those who pierce or tattoo their skin or wear unconventional clothing or simply dress stylishly and use their material possessions and consumer experiences to deliberately and consciously say something about themselves and their ideals. Radicals' inclinations to deny the impact of the symbolic meaning of goods are *pointless*—our goods act not just as tools but symbols; assuming that we live in society's mainstream and not in isolated subcultures, the meaning of our possessions will be constructed and will convey a message, whether we like it or not. In this we see one of the biggest differences between the followers of radical consumer Christianity and those of Consumptianity: the former act as though the construction of meaning in goods is an option (which they choose to not exercise), whereas the latter not only recognize the inevitability of meaning construction but embrace the opportunities it presents to communicate and enact their most deeply-held convictions.

In summary, Christians are apt to recognize the timelessness of Jesus' teachings while neglecting the same quality in his pedagogy. It is his educational technique of using common possessions to say something about his most deeply-held convictions—a technique that can be used across time and culture—that permits us to take Jesus consumer directives to hold no property, defend our possessions, carry no money, and generously share our and graciously receive other's possessions seriously, without taking them literally. Still, the question remains, "Should we take Jesus' consumer teachings seriously?" Or are Jesus' consumer teachings, as some have argued, merely antiquated rules that hold no relevance for today's modern consumer?

ANCIENT CONSUMER SOCIETIES

Modern research helps us understand the "meaning construction" process, but we are interested in something more. How did Jesus use goods to construct meaning in a world that predated modern consumer society by nearly two millennia? In Jesus' world goods were not in abundance, quite the opposite, and it would be a mistake to think that Jesus and his early followers had at their disposal, as is the case with most modern American Christians, a vast array of objects to choose from in order to construct new meaning to explain God's purpose on earth. Consumer historian, Peter N. Stearns (2006), explains that modern consumerism was not possible in the ancient world as technology, economic, and social conditions essential for consumer economies were missing. In Jesus' day, these included first, the demand for durable surplus, critical to consumer society, which could not be met in predominantly agrarian societies; second, widespread and desperate poverty, which made it impossible to build a prerequisite customer base who could afford goods and services; and third, a relative dearth of large cities, which hampered prosperity as well as the establishment of international markets and trade. But it was more than lack of a consumer technology and product distribution logistics that kept the ancient world from fostering consumer cultures. More fundamentally, it was because the idea of consumerism itself clashed with the predominant values systems of the old world. How? Stearns informs us, first, that the demand for novelty clashed with traditional social hierarchies and authority; second, that "this-worldliness" clashed with the otherworldliness of old world spirituality, detracting one from the true purpose of his life; third, that the "softness" of the consumer life clashed with the crudeness of the warrior, the disdain for refinement and the inclination for crudeness which was prevalent in the ancient world; and finally, that most of the dominant religions in the ancient world condemned material excess.

The absence of so many modern systems, technological and ideological, makes it virtually impossible for us moderns to simply lift ancient consumer instructions and habits, like those prescribed by Peter and the other New Testament writers, and apply them word-for-word to our lives in modern consumer societies. So, are Jesus' and the New Testament teachings, spoken and written in a culture predating modern consumer culture by hundreds of years, irrelevant, as James Robinson and other theologians have concluded? No. The fact that modern consumer culture was not possible in Jesus' day had no effect on his ability to use the goods he had at his disposal, meager and simple though they may have been, like any modern-day consumer, in ways that went beyond their literal use. As we have read, when it comes to faithful consumer behavior, the *process* of consumption is more important that the specific goods themselves. It's not the rat, cat, and dog themselves, but how our homeless friend has constructed a message of profound meaning with these animals. For Jesus, what were these goods and, more importantly, what procedures and processes did he employ to evoke meaning from them? What lessons are to be learned by watching the "You-Tube video" of Jesus' life?

Of all the consumer goods Jesus used to express his beliefs, which one stands out in particular?

The biggest rows between Jesus and his Jewish and Roman contemporaries, and among the early Christians had to do with a single consumer object and its consumption: *food*—when it was appropriate to eat, and when it was not (seen in the Pharisee's disgust with Jesus' disciples harvesting wheat on the Sabbath—The Gospel of Matthew 15:2); how much was appropriate to eat (seen in the Baptist's and other Jewish groups questioning of Jesus excessive consumption when it came to food and wine—The Gospel of Luke 7: 33-34); and, in the case of the apostles Peter and Paul, what a good Christian should and should not eat (in the epochal debate between both men on the role that Jewish food restrictions should play in the consumer and religious lives of non-Jewish Christians—The Letter to the Galatians 2: 11-21; The Acts of the Apostles 10). The debate between the Jewish and Roman leaders against Jesus became what amounted to an ideological tug-of-war between the two parties who represented, respectively, two different approaches—instrumental and expressive—to the consumption of food. The Romans and Jews wanted to use food instrumentally, governing its consumption according to strict religious and social laws. Jesus, on the other hand, desired to use food expressively to point to something larger than the bread and fish themselves, something much bigger than the petty prescriptions set down by the Jews and Romans for their consumption. This difference between Jesus and the Jewish and Roman leaders is a critical one as it strikes at the heart of the way the three parties saw society and its divisions. As such, it deserves further explanation.

JESUS, JEWS, AND ROMANS

Of all the things that these three parties could conflict over, why did food figure so large in the relationships between Jesus and the Jewish and Roman leaders? First, the Jewish leaders of Jesus' days exercised punitive rules that governed who were *invited* to eat with them. For the Jews, the "table of plenty" at which all were invited sit and dine, a principle metaphor Jesus used to characterize his mission on earth, was an affront to their belief about non-Jewish people and Jews who didn't follow the rules, rules which instructed that only certain kinds of people were welcome before God. Second, the table of plenty was an audacious challenge to the Roman system, for which the lack of availability of food and drink defined an elaborate social system designed to build up the rich while taxing everyone else into poverty. In other words, Jesus' invitation to all to come and eat violated the social contracts of the principle landlords of his day, terms that defined who was "in" and who was "out."

To us moderns, Jesus' demonstration of God's abundance in food and wine may seem to be a minor point of his ministry. But for Jesus' original audience—which included those (like himself, his parents, his siblings, and most if not all of his close associates) not invited to participate in the mainstream of religious and political society—it was his mission's centerpiece. And for the authorities looking on, Jesus' use of bread and wine was a serious threat not just to their understanding of the way society ought to be conceived, but also to their official positions and the influence they had gained by enforcing that understanding. By violating the Jewish and Roman literal application about the consumption of food, Jesus symbolically used food to herald a new movement with a new set of principles, much as members of a revolutionary political movement don distinctive uniforms and hoist newly designed flags. Why food?

Food was for Jesus' ancient listeners the modern equivalent of the middle-class American's home in the suburbs, his car, his steady and satisfying employment, his college degree, his paid vacation—consumer objects and experiences that embody and symbolize a good, rounded, abundant, and satisfying life. Why were Jesus and his class of people upset with Roman and Jewish leadership? Wouldn't most Americans be upset if a country invaded the U.S. and threatened their consumer lifestyle—took away their home, decided whether or not their kids went to college, determined how they would transport themselves and their family to home and work, and decided whether or not they would have sufficient food and drink needed to carry on a satisfying life? This is what the Roman invasion of Jesus' homeland meant to him and his peers—a lifetime of abject poverty over which most Jews and Romans had virtually no control. While we dream of the perfect world in terms of healthy marriages, secure retirements, and funded college educations, Jesus' peers dreamed: "If only I could *know* that I would always have food, life would be perfect." Banquets, stocked shelves, tables full to overflowing—these were Jesus' consumer object lessons used to explain and express his mission, ultimately coming together in a meal the night before his arrest, his last, in which would eventually come to reside for the Church an even broader meaning of Jesus' purpose (Eucharist). Peter Brown (1982) writes:

> Thought about eating was inevitably a form of second thought about society and its blatant divisions. In the world of the Mediterranean, the Kingdom of Heaven *had* to have something to do with food and drink. (Emphasis mine)

A question Jesus' dining behavior with food must have raised in the minds of the Roman and Jewish leaders was: "If everyone is invited to God's party, what role do our rules play, what role do we play? Indeed, is there a reason for our religious and political structures—our titles, rules, laws, and privileges—to exist at all?" Seen this way, the command to trust in God for all your necessities and be willing to help others and be helped by others with the necessities wasn't just some "feel good" blather. These were *fighting words* aimed at casting suspicion over the two most powerful landlords of Jesus' day. In the act of sharing bread freely to thousands no matter what their religious or political beliefs, Jesus essentially attempts to rewrite social-ethical programs, re-compose political and economic statements, and reconfigure religious purposes—not literally with pen and paper, but expressively with the simple consumer goods he had at hand. He did this not from his office at the top of Jesus Towers or from anyone's towers, but in discreet and hidden consumer practice spaces where his peers practiced their everyday consumer lives.

HOW TAKING JESUS' MESSAGE LITERALLY ENDS UP VIOLATING THAT VERY MESSAGE

Jesus modeled a life of mission that willingly and eagerly expressed the full process of meaning construction—all six steps, instrumental and expressive. Taking a well-known story—the "Feeding of the Five Thousand"—the instrumental meaning of the feast described is seen: The people are hungry (Step 1) and the only thing that will satisfy them is food (Step 2); so gather what food is available and ring the dinner bell—let's eat! (Step 3). This is notable. Not all (perhaps most) are willing, as was Jesus, to see hunger in their world and actually do something about it. But there is more than food offered at this meal: the loaves and fish express central principles of faith, which are that God does not abandon anyone in their time of need (Step 4); that God's ability to save us—from hunger, sickness, nakedness—is miraculous in a way that is no different than someone taking just two loaves and five fishes and successfully feeding thousands (Step5); and that God is willing to go to extreme, even miraculous measures to ensure that all are the recipients of undeserving and unconditional generosity (Step 6).

As we read earlier, many anti-consumption groups are willing to only go halfway, to Step 3. The fallout is immediate and easily seen in the beliefs of some groups whose literal approach to material possessions stands at the center of their lives, and often played out in insular communities, resulting in lifestyles and actions that have little impact and peculiar interpretations of divine teachings that hold even less relevance for most Americans. Misunderstanding by outsiders runs amok. By stopping the meaning construction process halfway, objects meant to symbolically express reconciliation for these radical consumer Christians are interpreted by others as signifying the judgment of non-believers; lifestyles designed to portray holiness and obedience are perceived as pompous; styles and habits meant to enact deep spiritual commitments are trivialized as pleasingly and benignly old-fashioned or just plain weird.[5] Lest we be too hard on only a few ultra-strict Christian groups, the temptation to withdraw from society in order to live literally the way Jesus taught is possible with any Christian group who believes that they have no hope of ever remaining faithful to Jesus and at the same time feeling at home in the world, its cultures, and with its material goods. You don't have to be a member of any particular religious group to make this assumption. The withdrawal from the Kingdom of the World, the attempt to follow his Jesus' teachings to the letter in order to be a really good Christian can be enacted anywhere—from isolated, rural faith communities to suburban track homes. Consumptianity asserts that the response to disengage from consumer culture or actively "jam" its technologies and categorically "diss" its consumer artifacts is anti-Consumptianity *and* anti-Jesus. Here's why ...

THE CRUX OF THE MATTER: "WILL I CHANGE OR STAY PUT?"

The message Jesus expressed in the events and experiences surrounding eating and drinking highlights *two central aspects* of his mission instructions, which can be described as dialectic between sameness and change. Jesus uses material goods to articulate two immaterial principles central to his mission, which are first, *continuity* in the face of change, reflected in his mission instructions to rely on God for all one's material needs, and second, *liberation* in the face of oppression, also seen in his mission instructions to be generous with others regarding the personal possessions one has gathered. To accomplish both, all six steps in the meaning construction process must be engaged. Do goods have a utilitarian purpose? Of course, but if that's all Jesus had limited them to he would have been merely a person who knew how to throw a great picnic, not a spiritual savior; a doctor not a healer; a social worker not a miracle worker. By going only halfway and refusing to plow headlong into secular society with a message of positive change and the intention to see it happen, by stressing continuity only in the literal, instrumental role of material goods, Christian radicals and some secular anti-consumption groups circumvent the instrumental *and* symbolic expression required for all-out physical and spiritual liberation that Jesus envisioned. But why—why do radicals refuse to go all the way, to move out and make themselves at home in the world, consuming all it has to offer with gusto and imagination? What is the primary motivation behind the radical's extreme disinterest in the things of the material world? Why have they focused their strictest interpretations to the very things—our food, our dress, our transport, our housing—which provide not only daily sustenance but also add deep and abiding meaning to our lives and relationships? In short, why are radicals some of the most "un-radical" people one could ever hope to meet?

GENEROSITY OR FEAR?

Ask most radical consumer Christians what is the biggest risk they take by embracing and engaging the material world and most will say it is the danger of compromising their beliefs. As we read earlier, it is a constant drumbeat in radical faith communities: indulge in the world's kingdom *at your own risk*. Scratch the surface and one sees, however, that the biggest risk for radicals, or any brand of Christianity, by leaving the security of their hideaway, protected communities and drifting, kicking their shoes off and making themselves at home in their resident culture and its consumer subcultures, has virtually nothing to do with their being seduced by the world's sinfulness. Rather, it has to do with being *exposed to the world's scrutiny*. The biggest risk for Christians willing to submerge themselves in the Kingdom of the World is not having their morals compromised but having the ideals they purport to embrace held up to public examination. As we read shortly, what really frightens radicals is the very thing that really frightened the religious landlords of Jesus' audience: uncensored, raw exposure. Not the risk of losing their religion or ethical ideals but the uncertainty of moving from secure and familiar places to unknown spaces teeming with strangers eager to examine the evidence, waiting to see if their suggestions on how to "decorate their apartments" are better than anyone else's—this is what scared the religious radicals of Jesus' day and of our own times. In short, the basis of the anti-consumption Christian's seclusion and judgment of the world, the lop-sided and awkward relationships they often have with non-believers, is not founded on generosity, as Jesus intended, but *fear*. At the root lies not a crisis of faith but of imagination; that is, the inability or unwillingness to imagine of a world turned upside down by consumer codes that ask us to feed the hungry, clothe the naked, and set free the captives. The reason the world is so messy and diabolical is it not because people have failed to live strictly according the teachings of the divine, but because Christians have failed—sometimes inadvertently and sometimes deliberately—to imagine how the Kingdom of God might come to life in their small corner of the Kingdom of the World.[6]

IF THE RADICALS HAVE A HARD TIME GETTING JESUS CONSUMER COMMANDMENTS RIGHT, WHAT HOPE IS THERE FOR YOUR ORDINARY METHODIST?

"Receive no money. Take no property. Wear no gold ...." Are these reasonable principles we should literally apply to our own lives? By the lifestyles they choose, most Christians—now and through the centuries—answer, "they are not." Nor are any other New Testament consumer instructions reasonable *as long as* they are seen as laws that Jesus and the apostles meant for us to take literally. As literal injunctions, they are virtually impossible to follow, but as guidelines for expressing faith in the material world, Jesus' consumption commandments are nothing short of pure genius, and completely do-able. Should we ignore these and a host of other extreme instructions about consumption issued by Jesus and the apostles seeing them, as do some, as antiquated and irrelevant sets of rules? Should we limit his teachings by exacting severe codes of conduct as guides for faithful living? Jesus' consumer teachings are by any Christian standard holy injunctions, revelatory, divine—why in the world would any Christian want to ignore a single one of them, why would any Christian want to suck the life out of them by reducing and restricting Jesus teachings to a set of punitive rules?

To their credit, radicals refuse to ignore them Jesus' teachings. Still, they don't get it. Bluntly, their stance is not much different than that held by people acting on their worst impulses. The reason racism and sexism, for example, are so difficult to break in secular society is precisely because of the literal reinforcement these ideas receive in the material world—housing, food, wealth, property—that keep people and groups frozen in their *places*, guaranteeing that nothing changes, never will. By insisting on inscribing their own moral categories to indicate acceptable and unacceptable consumer behavior, Christianity's most severe consumer radicals like the Jews of Jesus' day, are hardly any different than you garden variety bigot, operating from a base of fear, unyielding in their beliefs, intolerant of any understanding of the material world than their own. At the very least, radical groups are apt to fall prey to consumer habits and routines that are mind-numbingly orderly, safe, and imaginatively-speaking, barren—a pattern of consumption which, we read next, is very different from the one modeled and taught by Jesus, a style of living guided by five codes that ask us to: 1) Unhesitatingly accept the generosity of others, 2) offer unbounded generosity in return, 3) hold no possessions, 4) hold no money, and 5) carry no protection.

Chapter Four

Jesus Espresso

Does a "double skinny, half-caf" hold life's meaning?

Is there a consumer lifestyle that fits best with Jesus' teachings? Jesus' mission instructions set goals for faithful consumption, and in this chapter I use modern research to help us understand ways to implement them. Researchers have identified three predominant consumption patterns:

1. Straight-line Consumption
2. Spiraling Consumption
3. Stair-step Consumption (McCracken 1988)

Below, I describe each pattern and follow with a *real-life consumer* to help us see how these manifest themselves in their daily consumption of a single, ordinary product: coffee. We ask: "Which consumption pattern fit best with the practice of faithful Christian consumer behavior? Do any patterns help us practice Consumptianity?"

JAVA DRINKER # 1 (WENDY): PRODUCT AS ANCHOR [1]

First, *Straight-line Consumption*: The most conservative of the three patterns, straight-line consumption, evokes a pattern of behavior that regards possessions as anchors. The person's consumer goods, rituals, and experiences provide him with a straight *line of continuity* for achieving the practical goals of everyday life. To illustrate, we use not only an American staple: coffee, but a marketing staple, too: the focus group. Focus groups consist of 8-10 consumers and a single researcher whose principal goal is to uncover how consumers feel about their client's product. After a two-hour session, here is how one coffee-drinking consumer, Wendy, is described by the consumer researcher:

> Wendy has been loyal to Dunkin' Donuts since she first started drinking coffee twenty years ago. Each and every morning at 7:00, Wendy faces the same decision: whether to get in her car and drive to the nearby Dunkin' Donut store, or to make Dunkin' Donut coffee from the branded beans she keeps at home. Dunkin' Donuts coffee is more than an early morning activity. Wendy often grabs a second cup on her drive to work. Sometimes Wendy slips out during the afternoon and walks to the nearby Dunkin' Donut shop to purchase a cup of iced coffee. Wendy has a highly scripted morning routine, which she deviates from only with regret and emotional difficulty.[2]

Wendy explains: "Every morning I splash water on my face, I stick on shorts and a t-shirt, and I drive to Dunkin' Donuts. By that time the newspaper is delivered, I read my paper ... it's a 15-minute thing ...and then I start to make my lunch and by that time my coffee is done ... Then I'll make my bed, I'll take a shower, I'll iron my clothes, I get ready to come to work. This morning I didn't do my routine because of the interview (with you). *It was not easy.*" (Emphasis mine)

My response: "Wendy—get a life!" Yet you and I see aspects of our own lives in her attitudes and scripted rituals surrounding her coffee consumption experience. Like Wendy, our things, even the most ordinary items like a preferred brand of coffee, a favorite shampoo, or a well-worn Bible or prayer book provide a sense of who we are. Anthropologist, Grant McCracken (p. 124), writes: "Surrounded by our things, we are constantly instructed in who we are and what we aspire to. Surrounded by our things, we are rooted and visually continuous with our pasts."

All fine and good, but reading closely we see that Wendy's cautious attitude toward her possessions creates a sense of reassuring sameness that works for good *and* ill, restricting her to certain places, schedules, career decisions, recreation choices, and even the formation of personal relationships. A self-professed "control freak," Wendy denies herself the possibility of forming an intimate relationships because of the "consumption laws" she uses to support her need for continuity and control. She says: "I could never get married, never. It would drive me nuts to have someone tell me what to do or how to organize my life."

For Wendy, coffee and the ritual of consuming it go beyond refreshment. She uses coffee to gain and maintain control of her life. Coffee stands guard against unwelcomed people and goods who might interrupt her carefully planned life. People may not be dependable, but one thing's for sure, Dunkin' Donuts coffee will never let her down. McCracken offers an apt description of the insular life Wendy has chosen to lead: "Surrounded by our things, we are sheltered from the many forces that would deflect us into *new* concepts, practices, and experiences. These forces include *our own acts of imagination*...." (Emphasis mine)

So, is this what Jesus had in mind? Was he prescribing a mission lifestyle that commanded followers to gather products and experiences around themselves so that they could find in these possessions their identities, their stations in life, protection, and their emotional consistency? Well, no. Still it is probably true that Jesus enjoyed the "comfort food" straight-line consumption provided him in his small community in Lower Galilee. He may not have had a home of his own once he began his mission, but he clearly enjoyed visiting certain homes and families over and over again. He may have held no property, but everywhere Jesus looked he saw familiar real estate, goods, and associates. The synagogue in which he grew up, the businesses he and his family patronized, the places he gathered with his friends, the social fixtures and accouterments he had known since childhood—these were before him at every turn. He may have been homeless, penniless, property-less, and defenseless, but that doesn't mean that Jesus found no comfort or creative inspiration in the consistency that characterized his material world. To echo an earlier idea: Jesus respected this pattern of consumption; he just wasn't interested in employing it to bring about his mission, wasn't ready to throw personal creativity under the train; wasn't interested in prescribing consumer lifestyles for his followers that were tied to material possessions and implacable consumer rituals such as we witness with Wendy. Why? In short, this consumption pattern creates the types of places that make no room for *new* spaces. Wendy uses her possession to secure places where all are *not* welcome; where friends, lovers, and family members are strictly monitored less they upset the daily consumer routines of her life. What other patterns of consumption are available to Christians desiring to take Jesus' mission instructions seriously?

SPIRALING CONSUMPTION—BUT IN WHAT DIRECTION?

The opposite of straight-line consumption is a type of purchasing that moves from one purchase to another "without taking a breather." *Spiraling Consumption* is accurately associated with excess, but we limit its definition if we connect it only with materialism. Besides spinning upwards in a non-stop shopping binge, it can also funnel downwards into increasingly fewer goods and eventual poverty. This isn't necessarily bad. People often feel liberated as they divest themselves of material goods. Middle-aged couples like my wife and me, who downsize their belongings with massive garage sales after their children leave home, frequently shed previously experienced anxieties and restrictions surrounding the protection and care of their goods.[3] Similarly, consumers who engage in excessive charity and generosity open themselves to new thoughts, relationships, and yes, purchases, including gifts and self-gifts—possessions they previously could not have imagined for themselves.

Ironically, spiraling consumption is a common experience of monastic believers and others who have taken vows of poverty, permitting them to live at peace in mansions or caves, surrounded by diamonds or dirt clods. The excessive character of spiraling consumption can also lead to elevated levels of productivity and imagination. Artists, writers, entrepreneurs, designers, musicians, actors—members of America's so-called "Creative Class" (Florida 2006)—experience a sort of imaginative spiraling out of control that can extend to the material world as they encounter their greatest inspirations and create their masterpieces. Inventors, composers, artists, and designers gladly sacrifice their properties and fortunes to express their ideas, with hardly a thought as to whether or not there will be anything left to put in the bank at the end of the day. Do the most radical of radical Christians, like monks and nuns, get it right after all when they divest themselves of creaturely comforts, take vows of poverty, and live on the social and economic fringes? Did Jesus "spiral-out" when he permitted his disciples to receive no money and acquire no property, or, in an opposite fashion, when he permitted his follower to pour expensive perfume on his dirty feet (The Gospel of Matthew 26: 6-13)? Possibly—but probably not. That's because the pursuit of excessive poverty holds the same pitfalls as the pursuit of excessive wealth.

It is easy to identify problems that occur when consumption rockets upward into more and more possessions and consumer experiences. But don't the same problems present themselves when consumption funnels downward, thoughtlessly and at break-neck speed, into abject poverty? Generosity is one thing, but connecting one's very being and purpose in life to the material world—whether it leads to fabulous wealth or desperate poverty—is not what Jesus had in mind (John the Baptist—maybe, but not Jesus). Jesus didn't advocate severe self-denial any more than he endorsed materialism. He showed no interest in abject self-denigration, self-flagellation, or extreme deprivation. There have always been a handful of Christians, including many Christian radicals, who have been able to find spiritual fulfillment in extreme self-denial—God bless them. For them and the rest of us, it is nearly impossible to spiral downward without eventually running into the same problems associated with spiraling upward; namely, idolatry, which Webster defines as: "the immoderate attachment or devotion to a physical object."

Spiraling consumption, whatever direction it takes—up or down—is not what Jesus had in mind. That's because, for this type of consumption, it's all about the collection of places—as soon as one object is secured, another is quickly sought—as soon as one is divested, another is being sized up for Goodwill or a community flea market.[4] This pattern of consumption lacks an essential element: time—the time to reflect and attend to the responsibilities and enjoyment of owning and possessing, of disowning and disposal. Sociologist Elemer Hankiss' (2006, p. 122) study of "self-construction in the consumer age," asserts that "If time flows invisibly and emptily, if nothing articulates it, we suffer." Articulating time, he believes, requires slowing down. Up or down, spiraling consumption is a type of consumer behavior that does not permit the time and attention required to convert places into effective spaces, time to create meaningful consumption experiences, time to "say something" with our possessions about ourselves and our ideals. Does our final pattern pose some faithful alternatives?

ARE THERE CIRCUMSTANCES WHERE MORE, NOT FEWER POSSESSIONS HELP US FOLLOW JESUS' CONSUMER TEACHINGS?

When a couple is first married, it is often important for them to purchase new goods, not *just* because they individually need them, but because their life as a couple requires them. These new objects help weld a new identity—a "couple identity." They buy goods, services, and experiences that they never even thought of when they were single. As the couple gets older and brings children into the family circle, consumption demands increase: their son's interest in baseball builds a new "constellation of goods" that includes everything from stadium seats to sports gear to increased gas consumption to a new and larger van. Time passes and other events take place in the couple's life that introduces them to more consumer goods and experiences. Their aging parents' health care introduces them to medical procedures, legal services, and retirement centers. It compels them to make additions to their current home and buy books to help them understand the aging process. Researchers have a name for this pattern of consumer behavior: *Stair-step Consumption*.

Stair-step consumption is a pattern of goods acquisition and use that moves step-wise, it in "starts" at one point and temporarily "finishes" at another. Unlike straight-line consumption, stepping up to the next acquisition forces not only the adoption of a new set of goods but also the reformulation of new attitudes and the exercise of new behaviors. These goods and experience may be totally incongruent with the personal identity that the consumer has carefully nurtured and also may be inconsistent with the acquisition goals he has long held dear. That's why the disruption that stair-step consumption creates drives consumers like Wendy, with their strong need for control and consistency, to complete distraction. Is this a pattern of consumption that fits best with Jesus' ideas?

It's not perfect, but there are characteristics of the stair-step pattern that recommend its measured use for faithful Christian consumption. With this type of consumption, goods are in flux and set behavior gets shaken up now and then, usually for a good reason. Consumer experiences change, unlike what we see with straight-line consumption, but with reflection, purposefully—something noticeably absent in the spiraling pattern. Stair-step consumption permits consumers to break out of their "place-ness" and create new consumer spaces while steering clear of thoughtless and incessant goods acquisition or divestment. What provokes this pattern of consumption? What breaks the monotony of straight-line consumption? What halts the "spiraling shopper" in his tracks prompting him to slow down, take a deep breath, and wait for his purchasing and divesting activity to catch up? Stair-step consumption deserves special attention.

WHAT'S A "DEPARTURE PURCHASE?"

Stair step consumption happens when the consumer, who previously blocked the goods that didn't fit into his life suddenly, and sometimes without explanation, welcomes them. This sounds materialistic, and it can become so, but not necessarily. When new and previously unwelcome goods are allowed in, the consumer is forced to adopt new consumer attitudes and behaviors. Appropriately, consumer researchers refer to goods that force change as *"departure purchases"* (McCracken 1986). Using our previous example: After taking their son through three or four seasons of baseball, a couple is never the same. They purchase new goods and consumer experiences and adopt new ideas that are a direct result of their involvement with their child's sports activities. As they progress through the family life cycle, new consumption opportunities arise. Because of their experience with aging parents, new consumer spaces are created. A formerly politically-inactive couple suddenly becomes critical of social programs for the elderly they never before questioned; they explore different investment vehicles to secure their own retirement; they end up knowing more than many health care professionals about the peculiar ailments and pharmaceutical products that go hand-in-glove with growing older.

The purchase of baseball equipment, a new van to transport team members, long-term health insurance policies, plane tickets to visit aging parents, and other departure acquisitions—all can be seen as evidence of excessive and out-of-control buying. With their arsenal of possessions, middle class Americans are often criticized for their materialism. But this isn't always a fair or accurate judgment. What if their consumer behavior is simply reflective of people who have taken on the roles of responsible parents to their children, or of dependable adult children to their aging parents? How do we distinguish between responsible and irresponsible buying in this case? An important question to ask is: "What moves a person to make a departure purchase in the first place?" It may be tempting to conclude that the couple's consumer decisions about their child and parents are the outcome solely of clever advertising, product innovation, shrewd marketing, artistic design, persuasive salesmanship, promotional deals, so-called word-of-mouth advertising, and attempts to keep up with the Joneses. Anti-consumption advocates would have us believe this is what it is *all* about—bare-knuckled, smack down marketing. To some extent, they are correct. But they overstate the impact of business on consumer behavior and their knee-jerk, stereotypical beliefs do little to help uncover the true reasons for why we buy what we do. Is shrewd marketing the main reason Americans own so many things? There are at least three other forces that cause consumers to depart from old ways of purchasing and product use that have virtually nothing to do with Madison Avenue or competitive spending.

JAVA DRINKER #2 (ANNE): PRODUCT AS LIBERATOR

If we could identify the one thing that continually got Jesus in trouble with the powers that be, it was his incessant habit of introducing new ideas, attitudes, and behaviors, particularly about consumption. His fondness for *novelty* made his family and villagers uncomfortable and threatened both Jewish and Roman power figures and systems. That's because newness requires change; innovation demands questioning old and familiar ways. People who want to follow Jesus but simultaneously insist on staying the course are at cross purposes with the man and his message. New circumstances and unexpected events can provoke dramatic departures in consumption behavior, too. Can possessions act as catalysts for personal and spiritual liberation? Meet our second real-life, coffee-drinking, focus group consumer—Anne:

> Anne is in her early sixties, an administrator, divorced with grown kids, and has been consuming one cup of coffee per day for the last forty-five years—her preferred brand of coffee is Star Market, a high-end, relatively expensive gourmet blend. Star Market entered into Anne's life after a mid-life divorce that forced her to review her life and make some changes. In an interview with Anne, a market researcher asks Anne why she changed to Star Market shortly after her mid-life divorce.

Here is her response: "(I started drinking Star Market) because I was going through a sense of deprivation. I had quit smoking. My last child was out of the house. I lived alone. I had gained an enormous amount of weight. I had lost my source of income. I was really desperate. I didn't know where I was going to next. I was absolutely and utterly confused. I realized I was recycling all my same old patterns and thinking over and over again and getting absolutely nowhere (sic). I had to get off this cycle that was going nowhere."

The interviewer responds: "And gourmet coffee was a part of this big life change?"

Anne replies with a line any advertiser would love: "Sure. Gourmet coffee beans are all about creativity."

For Anne, a simple and relatively inexpensive departure product, coffee, serves to restore balance and a new sense of identity and meaning to her life after suffering a marital breakup. Mid-life divorce, death of a spouse, retirement, loss of a job—these kinds of disruptions often have an enormous impact on our everyday consumer lives. Frequently it is the case when we decide to make major changes in our lives that our old goods pathetically trail behind, sometimes dragging us back to old, ineffective consumer habits and routines. Newly converted Christians, exhausted by old patterns of consumption, find enormous relief entering into new relationships with people, places, and spaces that embrace and offer residence for new consumer goods, dreams, experiences, meaning, and priorities. Contrastingly, departure goods threaten people like Wendy, many Christians, and not a few churches who avoid them, maintaining the same predictable tastes, routines, and patterns year after year. But for others, departure goods come as a welcome, albeit somewhat scary, relief, helping to break down doors, sweep out old dusty rooms, break out of places into spaces, and propel them into a new and possibly more satisfying life. As Anne teaches us, the price of such goods is irrelevant. The experience of consuming even something as mundane and inexpensive as a two-dollar cup of Joe can help to affirm our inherent worth even when we feel completely worthless, get us out of the rut of our own small thinking, and help us claim a fresh and enthusiastic perspective. What other forces of change compel us to acquire goods—departure goods—that move us from places to spaces?

JAVA DRINKER #3 (FRANK): PRODUCT AS SELF-GIFT

Jesus understood the power of the gift. Christians agree that Jesus' life and death were his greatest gifts to humankind, but they often overlook the gifts he gave himself and encouraged other to give themselves. For those who express their Christianity in a lifetime of personal denial, sacrifice and anti-consumption attitudes, self-gifting may be perceived as contradictory of Jesus' severe consumer commands. Yet, self-gifting is a powerful act, having the potential to disrupt the endless and self-centered utilitarianism typical of straight-line consumption as well as the unreflective and exhausting buying and divestment behavior typical of spiraling consumption. Indeed, a willingness to give gifts to ourselves may reflect our willingness to be gifted by God, to admit our need for the divine, to "let go and let God." The power of the gift is seen in our third real life coffee drinker, Frank.

Frank is in his late 30's, a single, minimum-wage service provider who has consumed coffee for twenty-five years, 4-5 cups daily. His life is not easy—think dock worker, a Stevedore, the guy who cleans the toilets after your family finishes their Marriott weekend get-away. He explains: "I can't necessarily control what's going on around me. At times like that, you just want to go sit someplace, have a cigarette and have a cup of coffee to calm yourself and to relax, to be able to get back to dealing with what you have to deal with, to give yourself a break from all the stress around you so you can actually go back and deal with it again.

Frank's self-gifting extends into his after-hours. He says: "This is Hills flavored coffee, this is my special time. This (Hills Brothers) is my favorite coffee. A lot of times my cozy special times are when I'm alone at night. That's when my special coffee comes in, my flavored coffee. You know its' a little treat. It just makes a nice special mood for myself (sic) and I want to heighten that and give myself something special."

Frank, like millions of obscure, behind-the-scene workers, find in their consumer goods and rituals momentary relief from monotonous and unrewarding vocations. For eight or more hours a day, Frank is confined to a place, his place of work. Twice a day, though, he is permitted with the help of Hills Coffee to create his own space, even if for no more than 15 or 20 minutes at a time. What Christian would be so gnarly as to rag on Frank? Frank is precisely the kind of guy Jesus desired to assist—the little guy, the person operating behind the scenes. We don't need Jesus to tell us, our conscience will do just fine—if there was anyone who deserves a break, who could use a big, loving dose of generosity, who deserves a seat at the table of plenty, it's the "Franks" of the world. Jesus knew this and that's why this group of people laid such special claim to his heart. Jesus' personal enjoyment of his surroundings—his friends, their homes, a neighborhood eatery—may be seen as gifts to himself after a hard day's work, as places providing him the opportunity to create meaningful consumer spaces.

JAVA DRINKER #4 (SARA): PRODUCT AS IDENTITY FORMER

It's important to understand the inevitability of using our possessions to define our personal *identities*. A dear friend of mine and writer of several books on advertising, Dr. Richard J. Harris, is fond of saying that there are two myths about advertising: first, that advertising affects everything we do and second, that advertising affects nothing we do. Even the most radical anti-consumption advocate among us uses his possessions to say something about himself, even if that something is that he doesn't give a rat's keister about the clothes he wears or the cars he drives. Departure purchases permit us a degree of flexibility in our pursuits, help us to create a new identity and break with an unsatisfactory or unproductive past, and get on with the lives we believe God wants for us. Meet Sara, our fourth and final real life consumer (and you thought coffee was coffee was coffee): "Sara is a twenty-three-year-old Midwesterner who has recently relocated to the East Coast to pursue graduate school. Like others her age, she is preoccupied with the task of forging a distinct identity. Sara told us: "I want to establish (myself) as an independent adult person who is doing very different things from my farmer family." For Sara, the "farmer coffee" she grew up disliking personifies her rural roots she is so interested in breaking away from. She states:

> Coffee is something that people where I came from drink ubiquitously but it's this awful, weak, re-brewed farmer coffee. I used to serve that stuff every day… in a diner where I worked … to every old farmer with his conservative backwards views about the world. I never drank it when I lived there because I thought, Oooh, I don't want to be lower middle class and a farmer myself. No, I'm going to school to get an education.

Now, far away from home and in the city, Sara drinks high-end coffees, like Gevalia. By drinking Gevalia, Sara is able to distance herself from a past where the demand to fit in and "get with the program," stifled and suffocated. About Gevalia she says: "(It) is completely opposite of the coffee I had experienced as a child. (I drink Gevalia because) I think that it's a big part of separating myself from my family."

Two things about Sara focus our attention: she is young and she is a lesbian (information she volunteers later in the interview). Like millions of young people who leave home and move to new locations, Sara is society's brightest hope—hers is a future that knows no bounds—yet. Like her peers, Sara is taken up with forging her identity separate from her family of origin. A risk-taker, she is the kind of person Jesus sought and held up as exemplar (The Gospel of Luke 7: 44). A lesbian, Sara refuses to stay put, to be pigeon-holed in society's letterbox of outcasts. She won't settle for assuming the lesbian's *proper place* in the rural community of her childhood, with its rumors and small-mindedness; she wants to be free to go to new places in order to create new spaces. Much like the leper of Jesus day, people that landlords were inclined to fork-lift into their warehouse of human surplus, this gay woman hopes for more. Like the woman at the well, but in the reflective atmosphere of a coffee shop, cup in hand, we witness a young woman, scorned by many who believe they know what her place in life ought to be, setting down plans for new consumer spaces that will shape her life for years to come (The Gospel of John: 4).

CHURCH OR STARBUCKS—WHAT WILL IT BE THIS SUNDAY?

The meaning of our lives as we understand, construct, and re-construct it is, to use Jesus' words, "*at hand*"—just a cup of Joe away. It is in our everyday acts of consuming, at work or in a coffee shop, that we are afforded the opportunities to see, experience, and enact the Kingdom of God. For those who desire to follow Jesus' mission instructions, it is at these junctures—smack dab in the middle of the Kingdom of the World—that we are asked to take a risk, to infuse meaning into our consumer rituals, to find purpose in our goods and possessions, to form and firm our identities, to be generous with what we have, and to depart from old, tired ways. *This* is the profound and deep layer-meaning of life's trivialities. If it sounds daunting, keep in mind that Jesus did not drift alone, nor did he intend for his followers to take the loner's path.

In the next chapter (the last), I ask: "How do we implement Consumptianity into the organization of our faith communities?" But first, it is important to recapitulate the central argument I have made thus far. In a nutshell, I have attempted to establish that Jesus' consumer teachings possess the greatest potential to help us effect positive change in our personal lives and social relationships when we interpret and enact them symbolically, not follow them literally. The basis of this assertion, which is foundational for what I am calling "Consumptianity," rests on six things: 1) the findings of human cognition research that has shown that humans cannot be relied on to literally receive, remember, or follow any instruction because of their proclivity to interpret instruction in accordance with their personal needs, self-perceptions, and feelings, an inclination which ultimately overrides their need to get information accurately 2) the findings of consumer science which underline the fact that although people use their possessions as means to ends, they also invariably use them symbolically to say something about themselves, to assist in their self-definition, and to aid in the expression of their most closely-held ideals; 3) the response of Jesus, a person who was a devout Jew and who took the consumer teachings of his own religion seriously *without* taking them literally; 4) the difficulty of "cutting and pasting" rules from ancient onto modern consumer societies; 5) the weight of Church history which reveals that with the exception of a handful of believers, most (including the Apostle Paul), have followed Jesus' mission instructions in more of a creative, non-literal than a literal, by-the-books manner; and 6) the pedagogical style of Jesus whose primary tactic for introducing people to the Kingdom was to use common consumer objects (primarily food and drink) to point to something larger and more profound than the objects themselves, to ideals that, to enact and enliven, demand something more than a literal following of a set of rules. Having laid to rest the notion that the best way to take Jesus consumer instruction seriously is to take them literally, a concern for new consumption goals (not laws) is inevitable. It is to these and their enactment in communities of faith that I now turn.

Chapter Five

Jesus Corporate

What's the difference between St. Joe's and Joe's Bar?

"The notion that ours, inevitably, is a world in which production is of supreme urgency is an old one. So is the corresponding behavior. The discovery that production is no longer of such urgency ... involves a major wrench in our attitudes."
John Kenneth Galbraith in *The Affluent Society*, 1958.

"It is better to have a handful of enthusiastic advocates than hordes of people who appreciate your work—better to be loved by a dozen than liked by hundreds. This applies to the sale of books, the spread of ideas, and success in general and runs counter to conventional logic. The information age is worsening this effect."
Nasim N. Taleb, *Fooled by Randomness*, 2005

Every Saturday morning, truck farmers gather at a farmer's market near our home to sell fruits, produce, and crafts. One of these businesses is called "Jane's Farm." If Jane, the owner, decided one Saturday morning to go to the lake and go boating instead of to the market, would her company cease to exist? No, it would not. But what if Jane elected to sell her equipment, not plant any more crops, and no longer attempt to take any of her products to market? Would her company cease to exist then? Even though her company may still exist in name on a legal document, even though people may still inquire about her products and erroneously believe the company still existed, even though she still held a business phone number, business cards, a business checking account, and even though many of the trappings of the business existed, the business, "Jane's Farm," would indeed cease to exist.

WHAT MAKES A BUSINESS A BUSINESS?

Jane's business, like any business, whether it is a small farm or a multinational corporation, exists if and only if it conducts business. No matter how big it is or once was (until 2008, American investors could not imagine a world without Lehman Brothers), the minute a business ceases to do business it disappears. A business is not "A BUSINESS" but "a business," a collection of parts—people, financial accounts, equipment, and databases—whose existence is evidenced and defined by its interactions with those who consume its products, services, and ideas, and whose future is defined by its potentialities in consumer spaces where business is transacted and wealth is created. This is the case whether a business is run out of a city skyscraper or the back of a pick-up truck. If the parts are completely absent, the interactions and relationships between them disappear too, potential dries up, and the business quickly goes out of business. Does business exist as "a whole?" No, there is no Platonic ideal of business somewhere in space and time, but only active and interactive entities populated with individuals and groups of individuals who create value for themselves, their organization, their shareholders, and their customers as long as they interact with one another. How about a church? Does a neighborhood church exist as a whole? Can we correctly call the First Pedestrian Church, the CHURCH?"

WHAT MAKES A CHURCH A CHURCH?

Down the street from where I live is a marketing firm which is housed in what used to be a church building. Walking through the front door, it is not difficult to imagine where the altar used to be, where the parishioners used to sit, and where the pastor stood. It's easy to visualize what happened in the building, in certain corners of it, on raised flooring: babies were baptized, couples were married, preachers waxed eloquent, and caskets rested. Now where the pulpit was is a copy machine, where the organ stood is a glass wall office, and where babies were baptized, couples were married, and caskets were set is a worker's lounge. Does a church exist here? Once the parishioners left, the pastor moved on, committees disbanded, the financial books were settled, and all the contracts signed, sealed and delivered, it was over—the church continued to exist only in people's memories. This former church, like all faith communities, never existed as a whole, but only as a collection of parts that carried out its life in day-to-day religious and consumer rituals and behaviors.

Like a business, once a neighborhood church ceases to create spaces and becomes only a place, it is no longer a church—a marketing agency, perhaps—but not a church. I had a chance to witness this first hand while a seminarian in the 1970's. I was assigned the task of writing a paper on the inner city church, and so I contacted a number of churches finally coming up with three whose pastors agreed to meet with me. I have no memory at all about my experience with one of the churches (this was over 25 years ago), but my experience with the other two are still firmly in my memory. One was a 100-year-old church with a cavernous chapel that at one time provided space for 1,200 worshipers every Sunday morning. By the 1970s, the church consisted of 30 parishioners who met twice a month for Bible study. The second church, equally as old and big, was located in the same devastated neighborhood as the first, and from the outside the two buildings looked alike with garbage-strewn sidewalks, bolted doors, and indigent people waiting on the perimeter. The inside of the second church, however, was completely different from the first. The minute I walked in I was met with thirty to forty teens working on a service project. The place was abuzz with activity and I learned from the pastor that Sunday attendance ran over one thousand worshippers. Side by side this is what I saw: one church had become nothing more than a place; the other, a place teeming with spaces. The neighborhood church, like a neighborhood business, exists only as long as it successfully creates consumer spaces. Physical places, like first church, are nothing more than empty, lifeless caverns when active and interactive consumer spaces are absent. Their components—size, dimension, and costs—carry no import or meaning to the passerby.

There is such a thing as "the church as a whole," a spiritual ideal. Catholics call it "the Holy Catholic Church," (capitalized "C"), Protestants call it "the holy catholic church," (small "c"), and sectarians use a variety of names (e.g., "the community of the Holy Spirit"). These are more than titles but less than definable physical entities. Ultimately, the idea of the universal church is immaterial, a mystical ideal, far removed from the material world and the spaces where most take their kids to school and do their laundry. Members of the churches that Paul helped create understood their lives together sometimes as a whole—a spiritual entity—and sometimes as a collection of parts (e.g., the church in Rome). How are we to understand Jesus' group?

If today's churches were to use Jesus organizational model instead of Paul's, what would be different?

Jesus' group of twelve disciples was remarkable in that one would expect with such a tiny collection, each member would lean heavily on one another—that this interdependence would be a key characteristic of their life together, as was the case with the primitive and early churches. Instead, one sees with the Jesus' core a group of men who manage to steer clear of rugged individualism, but just barely. (Fishermen, carpenters—this was not a group inclined to ask for help.) The life of the disciple group is not a scaled-down version of Paul's church-as-body but something more akin to a modern business team, a group of independent contractors brought together to get a job done, held together not by their loyalty to one another but to the leader and his cause, directed by codes of conduct specified by the *ad hoc* mission at hand.

Like a business model, Jesus' organizational paradigm was not primarily defined by nor its existence dependent upon territory (as we'll read shortly, is the case with Paul's model) but by "potentialities," that is, its members ability to "conduct the business of God's Kingdom," in spaces as they came available. There is no reason to believe that Jesus saw his group as "a whole;" no reason to think that he saw the twelve disciples as anything but a group of people willing to leave their current employment and follow him. There is also no reason to believe that Jesus looked upon his disciples as "THE DISCIPLES" in some circumstances and "the disciples" in others, in the same way that Paul and modern Christians distinguished between the church at Rome and First Pedestrian Church when referring to a specific group of believers, and then use "THE CHURCH" when referring to something much bigger, more mystical, less tangible, more "whole" and less "parts."

We can only dream how the Church would be different had it followed Jesus' instead of Paul's model. The fact remains that Paul's analogy of the church as "a body," the body of Christ, has been *the* organizational paradigm for the Church since he wrote his letters. The model is interpreted both literally and metaphorically depending on whether you speak to this or that Christian, and it serves no purpose here to argue for one or the other approach. What is important is that we acknowledge the centrality of the idea for Christians that the Church operates as a group of interconnected people who, individually, are affected by each others' behavior. Indeed, one may conclude that Paul's organizational model stands on the same stage with Jesus' mission instructions in that both captured the most distinctive qualities of the movement at the time. The wisdom contained in both sets of teaching is timeless. What was the essence of the organizational model Paul prescribed?

Organizations that adopt an organizational model like Paul's (what researchers call a "functional model"—explained shortly) embrace three tenets:

1. They place the group above any of its individual constituents.
2. They value group integration over group conflict.
3. They understand that what happens to one of its membership is felt by all.

In short, with Paul's model, unity and agreement are essential. Negatively stated, the misstep of one is dire to the entire organization, placing the whole in jeopardy of total collapse—a plight about which today's small Christian faith communities of fewer than a hundred members or so are keenly aware. Unity and agreement were essential components of the early church's viability, threatened by its relative small size. Without these, Paul likely believed, rightly so, that the Church stood a strong chance of disintegrating.

Paul was not the first to conceive of an organization as analogous to the human body, and there is nothing uniquely Christian about Paul's conception of church-as-body. Social historians Howard Becker and Harry Barnes write that a functional understanding of organization, an organization-as-body approach, is "as old as social theory itself." Of their own examination of this model of organizational life, they write:

> We have already noted (the presence of the organization-as-body concept) in Hindu social thought, and have also called attention to the fact that Aristotle, in Book IV of his Politics, sets forth this ... analogy with precision and clarity. The same conception appears clearly in the writings of Cicero, Livy, Seneca *and Paul*. In the Middle Ages, (such an analogy was) drawn by John of Salisbury and Nicholas of Cues. (Emphasis mine)

A view of organizational structure and behavior as analogous to the human body, Becker and Barnes continue, was articulated by Hobbes and Rousseau in the early modern period, and, in the eighteenth and nineteenth centuries, by Hegel, Schelling, Krause, Ahrens, Schmitthenner, and Waitz. So why did this particular model work and why did Paul choose it in the first place? Did he mean for it to be *the* model for church organization for all time?

WHY DID THE CHURCH CHOOSE PAUL'S AND NOT JESUS' ORGANIZATIONAL MODEL?

The answer to this intriguing question is made clearer when we examine the evolution of the Church from its beginnings through the sixteenth-century Reformation. We identify five stages of development (below). We are particularly interested in how the Church organized itself in light of Jesus' consumer teachings and how obedience to these instructions affected Christians' relationship to the cultures in which they found themselves. We ask: Was there something inherent in the relationship between the Church and its resident culture that lent itself to a church-as-body model of organization during certain periods of the Church's history, and not others?

Stage 1 (30 C.E.): We title this first stage, *The Jesus Movement*. As mentioned earlier, Jesus did not employ a church-as-body model of organization with his small group, which consisted of one leader, twelve disciples, and fewer than a hundred mostly unidentified and poverty-stricken followers, wannabes, and hangers-on. The relationship of Jesus and his band of twelve to culture was mostly antagonistic, and the short life of the movement was marked by heated debate that often devolved into ugly and dangerous confrontation. At the heart of the tension was Jesus' "consumer commandments" to exercise unbounded generosity and hold no property, teachings that threatened Jewish religious exclusivity and the Roman economic and social class structure designed to keep the rich, rich and the poor, poor. If people took Jesus' consumer instruction seriously, these systems would likely collapse. Not surprisingly, the relationship between Jesus, his disciples, and the leaders of their day ended abruptly in Jesus' brutal execution, and eventually all twelve members of the core group were killed because of their allegiance to Jesus and his teachings. (While most Christians believe that Jesus' ministry lasted three years, most scholars agree that it lasted, at most, one year. The reaction of the powers-that-be to Jesus was not only brutal but swift, and their quick put-down of Jesus and his movement testify to the threat they personally felt.)

Stage 2 (31 – 40 C.E.): In the second stage of the Church's development, *The Primitive Jewish Church* (documented in the early part of the Acts of the Apostles), Christians numbered in the hundreds, possibly low thousands. Tension between the primitive church and the surrounding culture stemmed not only from its beliefs, but also its newness and its Jewish-ness (the primitive church was seen by Rome not as a separate and new religion, but a Jewish cult). Because members were predominantly Jewish, they were also monotheistic to the core and stubbornly unwilling to cow-tow to Roman polytheism or any religious program other than their own. The relationship between Rome and the Jews was extremely tense, and the violence toward Jews during the time Jesus lived in, according to some, was surpassed only by one other: the time of the Nazi regime in Europe. Roman leaders understandably wondered: How will we respond if this new movement gathers steam and moves against us? Extreme allegiance to Jesus' teachings (we may assume that many members had known Jesus personally) coupled with the communal lifestyles members fashioned in response ("holding all things in common"), moved the earliest Christians out of mainstream society and into a separatist, "us-against-them" relationship, exacerbating the tension already present between them and non-believers. This tense relationship between church and society still plays a central role in fundamentalist Christian groups who, espousing strong anti-consumption sentiments, often draw their inspiration from—and in the author's opinion, put undue stress on—a literal "enactment" of the communal life of the primitive church as recorded in the early chapters of Acts. Many such groups believe that if they are not in conflict with society, something is wrong with them, that they are not being truly faithful. For imbalanced groups, this misguided notion provides a convenient excuse to provoke solely for the sake of provoking.

Stage 3 (40 – 312 C.E.): In *the Early Church* stage (documented in the later part of the Acts of the Apostles as well as the Epistles), the Christian movement evolved into an organization of several thousand people after Paul began his ministry to non-Jewish people. The church-as-body model took on incremental importance with the addition of each new member. The belief that Jesus would return in a matter of days emboldened Christians in this period to be outspokenly judgmental of their resident culture, and it is also likely that Christians were perceived by non-Christians as societal "freeloaders," a group who contributed little to the present life, putting their energies into a world to come (according to their thinking) within a matter of days. Tension between Christians and their resident culture was formalized in Roman pogroms to hunt down, jail, torture, and kill Christians. We also see in this stage a willingness on the part of Paul and the writer of the Gospel of Luke to *not* follow literally Jesus' original mission instructions. For example in I Corinthians 9, Paul asks whether or not he and the other apostles do have the right to eat, drink, marry, and work for a living, adding an "expressive twist" to Jesus' consumer instruction to lead a life of poverty and receive no pay for their work. Similarly, the writer of Luke forgoes a literal interpretation of Jesus' consumer instructions (this some 70 years after Jesus' death) when, in his gospel, he has Jesus commanding his disciples: "if you have a purse, take it, and also a bag," and "if you don't have a sword, sell your cloak and buy one"—this being the exact opposite of Jesus' original instruction regarding money and in direct contradiction of his teachings on non-violence and non-resistance. This suggests that, by 70 A.D. Christians were not expected to literally follow Jesus' severe consumer teachings (although many still did, as evidenced by the writings of the early Church Fathers, like Tertullian, examined earlier).

Stage 4 (312 C.E. – 16th century): The State-Church stage came about thanks in large part to the efforts of a single man, Emperor Constantine. The State-Church arrangement included all citizens of the Roman Empire and numbered in the hundreds of thousands and, eventually, millions. The tension between Christians and their resident culture decreased considerably during this stage as the relationship between the Church and the State grew closer and stronger. This 1,000 year-plus arrangement tilted heavily in the State's favor and many Christians largely uninformed on matters of faith until after the invention of the printing press in the sixteenth-century, uncritically acquiesced to the viewpoints and demands made on them by political figures who added religious authority to their job descriptions. Jesus' consumer instructions were expressed in the context of Rome's political and economic hegemony, not individual communities of faith, with one exception: those radical Christians desiring to take Jesus' instructions literally, people such as St. Francis, who refused to operate in the larger society but carried out Jesus' commands in secluded communities removed from the cultural mainstream. Francis' group and others like it was, to be sure, not just small in numbers, it was miniscule and groups that have throughout history stood in the tradition of literal interpretation up to this very day have constituted and continue to constitute a mere fraction of the larger Church membership.

Stage 5 (16th century forward): The "Free Church" stage came about with a counter-Reformation movement originated by the Swiss sectarian reformer, Ulrich Zwingli. Counter-reformers formally broke not only with the Catholic Church, but also Martin Luther and other Protestant reformers. With few exceptions, the counter-reformers, adhering to Jesus' teachings on non-violence, bowed to the violent attacks of their Catholic and Protestant tormenters, and many passively went to their deaths offering no resistance whatsoever (cf.: *Martyrs Mirrors of the Defenseless Christians*—1660—by T.J. Van Braght). The Free Church movement ("Free" referring to the freedom between or separation of Church and State) represented an attempt to take Jesus' teachings seriously by taking them literally and, as with the first-century Church, this threatened the powers-that-be. In this case, those powers were not Roman or Jewish but Christian, namely, Catholic and Protestant. Intra-church conflict at this time was pitched: Protestants fought against Catholics, Catholics fought against Protestants, and both groups fought against Counter-reformers.[1] The Free Church movement and its support for the separation of Church and State, originally seen as counter-culture in Europe, ultimately gained passage into the U.S. mainstream in the eighteenth-century due to the leadership of American President Thomas Jefferson with the so-called "Jeffersonian Experiment," which advocated the separation of Church and State in the newly born country. (The original Puritan settlers, in contrast, advocated a Church-State union along theocratic lines).

We may conclude three things about the Church's development: First, that after Jesus' death, the antagonistic relationship between early Christians and their resident (Roman and Jewish) culture was augmented by the their understanding of the consumer teachings of Jesus that invited all, not a select few "to the table;" second, that these teachings contributed to a relationship between the early Christians and political and religious leaders that was tense and sometimes violent; and third, as will be explained more fully shortly, that this tension contributed to the Church's later adoption of Paul's model over Jesus'—a "defensive" model borne in a tough environment where the Church was daily threatened, and a model that valued strength and production and found it in increasing group size. This last point warrants explanation:

GROUP DYNAMICS IN TROUBLED TIMES

For the earliest primitive Jewish church—whose membership was small, homogenous, and under constant threat—numbers were equated with strength. A "united we stand, divided we fall" approach to group life also made a great deal of sense in the later small and struggling post-primitive/pre-Constantine Church (i.e., the Church of Paul and the Apostles) that was primarily populated with Gentiles who had never embraced a personal religion, much less a personalized religious experience in communities of like-minded people. For the later, predominantly Gentile church, consisting of people who had no religious history similar to the one shared by Jewish Christians, the sting of persecution when a member was imprisoned or killed was particularly acute, and for early Christians, both Jewish and Gentile, Paul's model which emphasized strength in numbers made a great deal of sense—but what about later?

After Constantine, the number of Christians grew into the millions, leaving little doubt that the Church would survive, if not thrive. By extension, we may infer that Paul's model held less relevance for the Church's survival after it was folded into the State, as it became bigger and stronger, and as it eventually represented military and political might as much as (if not more than) spiritual witness and moral integrity. The Church during and after Constantine could, for the first time, "play offense," not defense. Seventeen hundred years later, the Church remains unthreatened, particularly in free Western societies that have long separated the old Church-State union of Constantine and that see the right of citizens to practice their religion to be an inalienable one. Then and now, instead of contemplating its possible demise, the Church can focus on affecting spiritual and social change, not figuring out how in the world it will survive.

To now answer our earlier question of why the early, pre-Constantine Church chose Paul's and not Jesus' model, we reply: it is because Paul's church-as-body model, set against a violent backdrop where its continued existence was daily threatened by its small size, made more sense than Jesus' model, which gauged its strength by the unequivocal, no-holds-barred commitment of a few risk-takers to the "cause." In short, adopting Jesus' model in the life and times of Paul would have been a sure-fire way to destroy the early Church. Here an analogy to the business world may be drawn: In a tough business environment, small entrepreneurial ventures struggle mightily, unable to garner the resources necessary to fight the forces of inflation, unemployment, and lack of investment capital. Large corporations fare much better. Contrastingly, in relatively smooth economic times, small innovative businesses flourish having access to venture capital, low interest rates, and increased consumer spending (i.e., elements of a stable business environment.) Corporations do well in this kind of environment too. And frequently, in good times, instead of resting on their laurels, smart corporations take advantage of untroubled business climates to roll-out innovative products and to encourage an "*intra*preneurial" spirit (i.e., entrepreneurship within the corporation). In other words, during good times, big businesses often employ small business tactics. That's because the corporation's existence in good times is more or less assured and, consequently, its shareholders are motivated to move from a mode of survival in lumbering, unflappable, behemoth organizations to one of innovation, responsiveness, and investment. Like trying to build a new business in times of high inflation and unemployment rates, Jesus' model in Paul's time would have left the young Church enormously vulnerable to its opponents. And while each member of Jesus' original groups was murdered, including himself, the risk they assumed (considered foolhardy by any standard of organizational development) eventually paid off—as happens now and then with small businesses in tough economic times. Where do we find ourselves today?

Today, the Church in America and most of the western world finds itself in a safe environment conducive to innovative thinking and bottom-up entrepreneurial projects. Interactive and connective technology, such as the Internet, compliments today's "entrepreneurial churches," but contributes little to churches who desire to retrench, pull in, and cut their losses. In these times, the parable of the worker in the vineyard is especially poignant (The Gospel of Matthew 13: 44-52). Churches that bury their treasure instead of investing it exhibit, in the language of business research, "Type II error." Also called a "false negative" decision, Type II error occurs when churches falsely judge an excellent opportunity to be negative (i.e., too risky), electing to reject it out of hand and, ultimately, to walk away from near-certain success. Does Paul's model serve as the best organizational paradigm for churches in some climates (troubled times) but not others (smooth sailing)? Are some faith communities, like the Roman and the Jewish community during Jesus' time, making themselves less, not more accessible to all people when they insist on laying down onerous rules of consumption, laws that work well in sequestered groups under attack, but otherwise are viewed by outsiders as irrelevant, if not odd? Have churches elected to stay put in their little corner of the world precisely during a time, an unprecedented time, when a few of its members can with a little imagination, relatively small budgets, and the click of a mouse, provoke substantial positive change from one end of the of the planet to the other?

I argue next that Jesus' model makes sense in a consumer culture like our own. What the Church needs now, I maintain, is not a "production" model, like Paul's, a model where strength is equated with large numbers of Christians and where success is guaranteed by securing commitment to grand, large-scale campaigns to secure land and property and edifice, but Jesus' model, a active and interactive "consumer" model, where effectiveness is achieved in tightly focused, short-term, entrepreneurial projects directed by small strategic alliances of highly committed believers willing to use their imaginations and take risks with their possession and material goods. The "war" for the survival of the western Christian Church was won years ago; current and future "battles" to win the hearts and minds of people, I believe, start with a re-conceptualization of its organization. In a consumer society like our own that finds itself in the midst of an information revolution that allows a single person to effect more change in minutes on a $500 computer than landed and propertied millions were able to make in centuries, it is time to take a more serious look at Jesus' targeted, bottom-up, and work-on-the-fly organizational model. What are the components of such a model? We begin with a name change.

IF WE WERE TO ASSIGN A NAME TO JESUS' ORGANIZATIONAL MODEL, WHAT WOULD IT BE?

Christians often refer to their communities and gatherings as assemblies. Let's turn a few letters around and call the group that Jesus created "an assemblage." What exactly is an assemblage? Assemblages (the term originated in Gilles Deleauze' 1991 *Empiricism and Subjectivity*) consist of three components:

1. *Processes,* which articulate how groups are defined territorially,
2. *Roles,* which help define how groups are expressed internally and externally, and
3. *Codes,* which embody the standards by which groups enact their missions.

Let's examine each of these components in relation to Paul's and Jesus' organizational models. Specifically, let's address the question: How does Paul's "assembly" compare to Jesus' "assemblage?"

First, processes: A key component of assemblage theory is the idea of territoriality. For today's churches, the process of group identity formation is directly connected to their physicality, including their actual locations, property holdings, and the number of people associated with them (e.g., members, employees, clients, etc). When Christians say that they attend the church on Ninth Street, they unwittingly define their faith community in territorial terms. Similarly, when believers measure the success of their faith communities geometrically by the size of the church budget, the number of construction projects underway, or membership growth, they use territoriality to understand and articulate their personal and communal identity as Christians.

How do Jesus' and Paul's organizational models differ in their understanding of territoriality?

Territorially speaking, the organization of today's churches bears virtually no resemblance to the organization of Jesus' disciple group. Indeed, there is no evidence to suggest that Jesus or the very earliest primitive Jewish church used physical territory and geometrical measurements to define who or what they were. On the other hand, the early (post-primitive) Church under Paul's leadership and the later Constantinian State-Church with religious/political leaders at the helm *not only expressed but stabilized* their identities territorially. How did the notion of territoriality change in later church history?

As we read earlier in the five stages of the Church's development, territoriality expressed in a formalized Church-State union defined and stabilized the identity of the Church for 12 centuries before and during, and for 2 centuries after the Protestant Reformation. Infant baptism automatically "made" the newborn a Catholic or a Protestant depending on the territory in which its parents lived (of course, today, infant baptism carries no such meaning for Catholic and Protestant Christians). All were satisfied except for the newest kids on the block, the counter-reformers, the Anabaptists, who had no stake in either the Catholic or Protestant Churches or their territories. Dividing Europe into Lutheran and Catholic principalities was something that these sectarian radicals, taking their cue from Jesus group of twelve and primitive Christianity found no biblical support for and consequently opposed. One act in particular—adult baptism as compared to infant baptism—practiced by the counter-reformers posed a direct challenge to the Catholic and Lutheran idea of territoriality and faith, subverting the very notion of "Christian identity-by-territory" upon which Lutheran and Catholic princes built their power. Thus, during the Reformation, the counter reformers' advocacy of adult over infant baptism constituted both religious *and* political statement that signified a direct threat to the territorial systems that defined and stabilized Catholic and Lutheran religious, political, and economic identity and viability. In short, adult baptism threatened to destroy the *places* constructed by the Catholic Church over the previous millenium and the newly formed Protestant Church that had just begun to build influence and power in its own land grab in 16th century Europe.

In a Church environment that judged success territorially, members' financial aspirations weighed heavy. As Max Weber pointed out in his classic *The Protestant Ethic and the Spirit of Capitalism*, the religious decision by 16th-century Catholics to convert to Protestantism was frequently made for personal economic reasons. Many Catholic business leaders, for example, were drawn to Luther because of his support for usury, that is, the loaning of money on interest—something the Catholic Church had opposed for hundreds of years. In Protestant territories as opposed to Catholic ones, people's business ventures and personal fortunes were afforded a ready-made environment for growth and wealth creation. With so much at stake economically and politically, it is no wonder Luther and Catholic princes gave sectarians so little room to move—after all, if the Anabaptists got their way, which would have essentially de-territorialized both the Protestant and Catholic Church, then the ways of countless business people, Church officials, and political functionaries stood a very good chance of being destroyed. People so threatened will kill—and kill they did.

That was yesterday. Today, U.S. churches exist in a "free church" society where Church and State are separated and Christian denominations are not defined by Catholic and Lutheran principalities (such territorial markers still exist in parts of Europe, but in name only). Nevertheless, many U.S. churches—Catholic, Protestants, and even modern sectarian—still align their group identity with a physical territory, akin to say, a sales region. For many American churches, strength is measured geometrically, and territories (e.g., dioceses, districts, congregations, denominations, and so forth) act to stabilize their group's identity. Success for these churches, like that for Catholic and Lutheran principalities in the sixteenth-century, is defined as that which increases the church's physicality—its territory, the number and size of its places—and is therefore measured geometrically. This approach, a strength-in-numbers view that is based on an "over-reading" of Paul's and an "under-reading" of Jesus' organizational model, I believe is dated. I argue that by adopting Paul's at the expense of Jesus' model in today's climate, the Church sets itself up for the proverbial pratfall, adopting goals and employing tactics that grow increasingly irrelevant, especially to young, educated, and tech-savvy consumer Christians eager to effect change and make a difference. As was true for the Jews and Romans of Jesus' day, the question of "who's in and who's out" still takes center stage, still determines the success of the Kingdom on earth. Jesus' had an answer to the question, so what was it?

WAS JESUS INCLUSIVE?

In its quest to bring the Kingdom to life, is it better for churches to solicit the assistance of hundreds of average citizens or a dozen highly skilled and gifted people? Did Jesus pick his group with set standards in place, or did he simply fling open the door and let anyone interested join the cause? First-century Jews were not of a mind to throw open the doors to anyone save their own. Jesus was a Jew and a strongly monotheistic one at that. As much as we modern Christians would like to think of Jesus as inclusive, accepting, and inviting to anyone who happened to show up—well, he wasn't, at least not all the time. For every "woman at the well" (a social outcast that Jesus welcomed with open arms) there is a "rich young ruler" (a person on whom

Jesus exacted severe conditions of acceptance and who, consequently, turned away from Jesus' offer to sign up for his cause). Unsettling though it may be, Jesus selectivity and stringent conditions of acceptance probably contributed to the success of his movement, permitting him to choose only those he thought had the gifts, skills, and temperament to bring the Kingdom of God to life. Jesus' exclusivity especially riled the Romans whose tolerance of individual differences far surpassed anything seen so far in the U.S. or, for that matter, in world history. In short, Jesus' standards for his followers were, as evidenced by his mission instructions, excruciatingly high and the demands he placed on the lives and consumer lifestyles of those who would follow him were severe and uncompromising.

One "term of agreement" that for Jesus was non-negotiable was the territorialization of his movement. Jesus exercised his leadership, much to the dismay of his disciples and the disbelief of his religious peers, by deliberately *"deterritorializing"* his movement. He criticized places and "landlords"— Promised Land real state, Temples, and Offices; employed expressive and internal not literal and external measures of faithfulness; and chose to operate in temporary, extemporaneous spaces guided by discreet codes of conduct rather than in prominent, revered, and permanent places structured by hard-and-fast laws. Just as Jesus moved from space to space, so did his disciples, and as we read earlier, there is no indication that Jesus ever intended to construct a building to house his movement.

Second, *roles*: At that time Jesus went through the grain fields on the Sabbath. And his disciples were hungry and began to pluck heads of grain and eat. And then the Pharisees saw it, they said to him, "Look, your disciples are doing what is not lawful on the Sabbath" (The Gospel of Matthew: 12).

The roles that people and groups play in organizations are complex, but not unwieldy when we frame them in relation to their material expressions, as internal versus external. Jesus articulated the *role* of materials, objects, and consumer goods in his mission by going beyond the external material— flour, yeast, and water—to the internal "residence" expressive of high principles and ideals—abundance, spiritual sustenance, and salvation. When Jesus' peers, such as the Pharisees looked at a stalk of wheat, they interpreted it as ... a stalk of wheat. Like many radical Christian consumers, and like many secular anti-consumption groups, the Pharisee's purely external viewpoint provoked them to create rules, including many consumption laws, for which literal obedience was (could only be) measured externally and often geometrically in the cold light of observable behavior, visible to the naked eye. Looking at the very same stalk of wheat, *Jesus saw more*, not just the physical, material object but its immaterial expressions, visible to the discerning eye. With the material world, Jesus saw the expression of God's generosity, an openness that inspired believers to be forthright in stating their needs and willingness to receive as well as a graciousness that prompted them to give generously to those in need, which brings us to our final component of assemblage.

Third, *code*: When Jesus allowed his disciples to harvest grain on the Sabbath, he expressed the practical importance of filling a person's belly. But also, he articulated the primacy of expressive code that supported generous consumer guidelines over punitive consumption laws so strict that the "good" religious person was advised to ignore even a starving person rather than risk breaking the law and offending God. Jesus drifted from space to space, guided by consumer codes characterized by their flexibility and novelty, not rigidity and tradition. As a Jew, relationships for Jesus were defined and directed by the idea and practice of covenant, which, in Jewish history, prized loyalty over rational-legal contracts that demanded the fulfillment of strictly agreed-upon terms. His disciples adhered to his mission instructions primarily because of their loyalty to him and his cause, not because of their interdependence upon or personal commitment to each other—they had "signed" a covenant with Jesus, not each other, and they never signed a legally-binding contract with anyone, not even their leader. In summary, Jesus debunks consumption "laws"—whether issued by Roman and Jewish authorities or their modern-day anti-consumption counterparts—substituting them with consumption codes. These codes—to give and receive generously, hold no money or property, and refusal defend oneself and one's property—borne out of his mission instruction in the Gospel of Matthew 10—were neither geometric nor physically measurable. Their practice and effect were often "under the radar." They issued not from religious edict, but from "within," moving from the heart of a person and materializing in his interactions with others in shared consumer spaces.

WHAT MIGHT A MODERN ASSEMBLAGE LOOK LIKE?

The Church has chosen to create assemblies, not assemblages. But what if local churches today decided to use Jesus' organizational model instead of (or perhaps in addition to) Paul's?[2] What might they do? *First*, they might stabilize the group's identity by de-territorializing it, by gradually but steadily moving its primary (but not necessarily all) activities from physically-defined places—buildings and offices—to off-street spaces, such as alleyways, public parks, shelters, city squares, public buildings, bus depots, roadside rest areas, train stations, public beaches, hospital emergency rooms, and airports—places where members would be afforded the most opportunities to feed the neighborhood homeless, heal the physically and emotionally ill, and help free people imprisoned by their own emotional and spiritual diseases and scars. *Second*, churches might deliberately and systematically relinquish select contracts and divest certain church-owned property. The decision criteria for such moves would follow the life of the discipleship group. Where possible and most effective, the church would replace owned with rented property that included month-by-month leases which could be easily broken, affording the faith community and its members maximum flexibility to move about, wander, and respond to the physical, emotional, and spiritual needs of people in and outside their faith community. *Third*, churches might turn their de-territorializing campaign to private property—such as property estates, farmland, houses, and business buildings—owned by church members. Not all, but some members may conclude that is in the best interest of the Kingdom cause to sell their family homes and secure temporary rental housing, preferably in neighborhoods where they could easily assist the sick and dispossessed and that would, simultaneously, provide services that meet their family's essential consumer needs and wants. Church members may be encouraged to focus their primary attention on the ways they use and consume the houses and real estate they believed they absolutely need to own. Do their consumer habits and patterns further the cause of the Kingdom? Do their consumer actions maximize the use of personal and leased property to bring about the physical well-being, spiritual liberation, and emotional health of others? These are central question for directing church members' product acquisition and divestment behavior.

On a whimsical note, a coalition of neighborhood churches may choose to hold a series of meetings designed to show members how to *think differently* about the things they possess, their relationships to each other, and the people at work and in their neighborhoods. As a special guest, they might invite the dog-cat-rat man (along with his dog, cat and rat, of course) with the goal being to get members to engage their imaginations when it comes to living their lives on the street or anywhere else that finds them in the middle of the Kingdom of the World. A central theme of these meetings would be the importance of church members to *see beyond* what is apparent to most. To accomplish, audience members would be encouraged to assume an internal, not external approach to relationships and material goods, and be shown the importance of discerning the intentions of the person and not judge someone solely by his behavior and his stated attitudes. The meetings would include an underlying theme: how to divest those possession members absolutely do not need to own and how to employ a healthy dose of imagination with the things left over. Members might be encouraged to ask how they might use their bicycles, cooking utensils, clothing—all that they own—to bring health to the physically ill and liberation to emotional, physical and spiritual captives. Church members would be encouraged to ask: "What do I *say* to others when I wear that blouse, shop in that store, and take this type of vacation? How can I creatively employ the few possessions I have to convey a message of hope, like the dog-cat-rat man?" *Finally,* church members would be encouraged to ask what it means for their material lives to live not by consumer law but consumer codes, according to the five codes of faithful consumer behavior revealed by Jesus' mission instructions.

WHAT WOULD BE THE ROLE OF ASSEMBLAGE LEADERS?

> They said to him, "Let us sit in your glory, one on your right and one on your left." Jesus replied: "(I) did not come to be served, but to serve" (The Gospel of Mark 10).

Jesus' leadership was charismatic and his organizational structure was competence-based. Jesus' words were eventually seen as authoritative, but while he walked the dusty roads of Lower Galilee, while he built his assemblage of disciples, *the man, Jesus,* was perceived and received by most as just another Jewish prophet (i.e., the jury was out). Even his own disciples in the early part of their time together saw Jesus as one among many they could choose to follow, someone who, in their eyes, could best validate his mission by his competence. And Jesus obliged, validating his mission in miraculous acts of healing the sick, exorcising the possessed, and feeding the hungry. In short, Jesus was seen and comfortable to be seen as a specialist, not an expert; someone who was valued for his competence, not his authoritativeness. Consumptianity asserts that churches that adopt Jesus' assemblage model of organization are led by specialists, not experts, who value competence above authoritativeness. Who is the specialist?

The specialist limits himself to talking about what he knows. Specialists have a specialized language, one of their distinctive characteristics, that permits them to talk, think, narrate, and compose in ways that are not at all like the language of non-specialists. For the pastor, the task is to translate their lexicon, education, intelligence, and competence into the daily lives and everyday activities of ordinary people, non-specialists. Pastors, along with many other leaders (like Jesus), are under constant pressure to speak and act authoritatively and they are often tempted to conduct this translation from a position of authority, something that Jesus, the man, was wise enough to not do. The pressure to assume an authoritative position often comes from followers who have not the courage or imagination to drift and compose their own stories, who demand a "no painting the walls" clause. To use psychoanalyst Erich Fromm's words, many Christians (past and present) yearn to "escape from freedom," preferring, instead, the captivity of authoritative leadership directed by intractable dogma that instructs them about how to be a 100% guaranteed good religious person (an absurd and pointless mission, as Jesus pointed out to his power hungry disciples in the passage above). As soon that the pastor ceases to be merely an expert and becomes the authority, he replaces the bag of moves and tactics that he can legitimately lay claim to with a "property of authority," which he is not qualified to possess. His, in the words of de Certeau, is "a simple case of mistaken identity."

ASSEMBLAGE LEADERSHIP: THE BOTTOM LINE

What do the "specifics" of assemblage leadership entail? *First*, leaders must remind themselves that Jesus' purpose in life was to feed people, not become the Minister of Food. They do well to warn themselves and each other of a strong and persistent tendency on the part of followers to give them, their leaders, more credit than is due. Following Jesus' own behavior, leaders would consciously and deliberately choose competence over authority and consistently discourage church members from ascribing authority or anything beyond simple expertise to anyone in their faith community or in the broader church community. Instead of permitting themselves to be drawn into the social and political demands of a person regarded as "the authority," church leaders would do well to take their cue from Jesus who purposely chose to operate "beneath the radar" and enact his most notable achievements far from an adoring and obsequious audience, in inconspicuous spaces. As happened with Jesus, leaders could anticipate that when they refuse to act authoritatively, some followers will leave and turn to other leaders, ingratiating landlords, who will eagerly oblige their desire, a very human desire, for faith minus uncertainty, religion absent the awkwardness and personal discomfort of a leader who rejects a bigger-is-better approach and insists on working in the cracks.

Second, church leaders hoping to lead assemblages will want to remind themselves that that while they are gifted, they are not special, and that ultimately, they use the same bag of moves that are used by their parishioners in their accomplishment of daily living, only slightly garnished with a sprig of specialized competence. Chosen leaders may decorate their own apartments with a bit more taste and finesse than most, but that's about all they do. They may, like a pious monk, pray every two hours round-the-clock, but, ultimately, their lives happen "in the meantime," or as composer John Lennon once said, for us: "Life is what happens while you are busy doing something else." In short, leaders do well to remind themselves that they are nothing more and nothing less than a consumer. As long as they act simply as specialists, not experts, they enact their calling to help people manipulate and create, making suggestions in line with the maneuvers and tricks that they have managed to acquire through the rigors of training and the experiences of life.

PARTING SHOTS: HOW THEN SHALL THE CHURCH OPERATE IN MODERN CONSUMER SOCIETIES?

The struggling primitive Jewish church and the early pre-Constantine church found themselves in a time and place that were conducive to gauging their strength extensively (geometrically), not intensively. Their conception of the world and the Church's place in it may be described as a "block universe," *a whole* entity that could be sized up and measured (cf. Bourdieau's seminal book, *The Order of Things*, which explains how this conception of the world dominated Western society until the sixteenth-century). Jesus saw things differently and articulated his mission in terms of potentialities and capabilities, not production, volume, and formulae. His model was based on the premise that one could potentially accomplish more with 12 than 1,200. He was not the only one to employ this strategy. Businesspeople have known for years that "eighty percent of the success of an organization comes from 20% of its consumer base," the so-called "Pareto Rule." I have argued that is important in modern consumer society marked by freedom of religion and the free spread of ideas expedited by high-tech isn't the long-term sustainability or protection of a religious group let alone its ability to produce and grow into an enormous organization, but the commitment of the core to the imaginative diffusion of Kingdom ideas and ideals, and the leader's ability to inspire through the persistent and consistent announcement of that cause, accompanied by a sensitivity to the consumer spaces where this is most likely to happen.

The idea that I am proposing—that growth and production should no longer be the mainstay of the Church—is difficult to swallow and would, if taken seriously, be heartily resisted. For centuries and especially in today's U.S. churches, Christians have followed the rule that whatever increases membership, giving, and physical plant is good, and that whatever does not increase the productive capacity of the Church is bad, possibly evil or at the very least, unfaithful to the missionary mandate and possibly a sign of unfaithfulness on the part of members. At the local level, the congregation that never grows beyond a hundred or so people and never oversees a million dollar budget is apt to be viewed as having something wrong with it. In contrast, the congregation that has hundreds and even thousands in attendance and has its eyes set on expansion at every conceivable level is seen as being blessed by God. These are unreasonable ideas, both in their conception but especially in their expectation. Judging churches that are small to be bad and large ones to be good casts a wide net of castigation given the fact that 59% of all churches in the U.S. have fewer than 100 members, some as few as seven (Hartford Institute of Religion Research, 2008). These churches—those that "must be doing something wrong"—include 177,000 congregations and provide church homes to 9 million worshippers every weekend!

And what about the congregations that must be doing something right, the ones with lots of people in the pews, say, more than 1,000? Now we are talking about a mere 2% of all U.S. churches, the majority (approximately 94%) being Catholic and the rest, Protestant mega-churches. What a presumption to make: that only 2% of all U.S. church-goers "get it right." Are we then to conclude that fully 98% of American churches constituting 294,000 churches and 43 million worshippers "get it wrong?"

This way of thinking about the Church, as Max Weber pointed out a century ago, is the child of economic theory grounded in America's distinctive brand of capitalism which, like most brands, frequently benefits only a handful of people (religious brand managers, if you will) who, like their corporate and political counterparts, are rewarded when market share grows and fired when it doesn't. But even Weber's critique seems dated and unnecessarily complex for the culture of high-tech consumerism we find ourselves in today. There is a single and simple compelling reason to reject the production-oriented approach of the past and that is that it grows increasingly irrelevant, especially for the most recent generation of American young adults. What relevance does the production model of church organization designed to expand no matter what the cost hold for the young businessperson who has spent four years of his life in business school learning how to make an organization super-efficient and who spends the better part of his working week finding ways to cut back, build product value, and grow market share within the strictures of his budget? How does a young couple struggling to pay their food bills and use their homes to their utmost efficiency relate to a massive church edifice that stands empty for the better part of the week, waiting for them to enjoy for one or two hours on Sunday morning? How do today's young educated people whose generation is marked by high levels of concern for the environment reconcile the carbon footprint left every minute by a multitude of church plants and campuses? What is a young, professional worker, who works and conferences online at home each week and visits the corporate offices once a month, to make of Church leaders flying across the nation and globe, conducting meetings with a dozen or so officials, accruing daily hotel and restaurant expenses in the thousands? Last but not least, what does the future hold for large church organizations packed with a generation of consumers whose loyalty to everything from a brand of cereal to a specific faith community is the lowest seen in American history?

Church leaders, like political and business leaders, succeed when they generously and graciously direct short-term alignments and coalitions with like-minded people and groups, creating something beyond what they, alone, or their group, alone, can even imagined, let alone construct. The Church, like its corporate and government counterparts, sees its greatest successes coming not from the hard work of thousands, but the coalition of dozens inspired by the imagination of a few competent leaders, fueled by the capacities and potentialities that take place in the on- and off-line interaction of a handful of individuals and groups bent on achieving goals whose implementation happens not in a thousand acres of brick-and-mortar edifice, but in consumer spaces here one minute and gone the next, consciously chosen and deliberately fleeting. The organizational model that is most likely to increase the possibility of this happening, of affirming the value of each congregation no matter how large or small, I believe, is not found exclusively in The Letter to the Romans but also in The Gospel of Matthew, in Jesus' mission instructions on how he wanted his group of followers to consume.

Conclusion

The world Jesus entered in 30 C.E. offered rooms for rent that were framed by thick, heavy boards (i.e., religious beliefs and practices) that had been nailed down by two fasteners: the Torah and Jewish tradition. Today, Christians rent rooms that are fastened down with the nails of tradition and Holy Scripture, too. But any referential power tradition and scripture once held for Christians has been in a slow but steady state of decline for the last two millennia, leaving believers with rooms in bad need of refurbishing, if not complete repair. In the absence of powerfully strong and anchored referents—the stuff of spiritual heritage—today's Christians rent rooms that are fastened with a little bit of this and a little bit of that—the stinky stuff of culture—tape, wire, fish carcasses, used syringes, beer cans, seaweed, and other flotsam and jetsam that washes up from their T.V. sets, theaters, fashion runways, blogs, car showrooms, chat rooms, and a brown sea of American pop culture as distinctive as the taste of fire-dried hops in a glass of Kentucky Bourbon. This is the brown swill Jesus called the Kingdom of the World, the place Jesus asks us to settle into, not avoid, to get comfortable with, and consume with abandon.

While Madison Avenue exerts strong control over millions of consumers' lives, ultimately, people control how the goods they possess will express themselves and their ideals. Although Jesus' severe consumption codes can be followed literally to set Christians apart from the Kingdom of the World or to oppose the very idea and practice of consumerism, as such, they fall well short of the potential he envisioned. What is possible? In today's terms, how might we re-interpret Jesus five "consumption commandments" for the sophisticated consumer culture in which we live? How do we practice unbounded generosity, graciously receive from others, carry no money, possess no property, and refuse to defend ourselves and our material goods without demanding of ourselves and others lives weighed down by onerous and restrictive laws of conduct? We do this by using the material possessions with which we have been gifted to:

Cultivate standards of excellence, personal ideals, and aspirations.
Create new consumer lifestyles as well as sustain old ones worth sustaining.
Change how culture and cultural artifacts are represented.
Shape, transform, and enliven accepted perceptions of the world and our relationships in it.
Aid our self- and collective identity.

Each directive exists as an opportunity to go beyond the self-evident. Each compels Consumer-Christians to move beyond the instrumental to the expressive meaning of their possessions. Each possesses the potential to turn ordinary and mundane places into extraordinary, possibly even miraculous spaces.

Notes

PROLOGUE

1. According to the Hartford Institute for Religion Research, there are 335,000 Christian congregations in the United States. Fifty-nine percent of U.S. congregations have fewer than 100 members and the median church size is 75. Approximately 118 million Americans (or 40%) of the population attend church. The average Sunday attendance for Catholic congregations is 715, 127 for mainline Protestants, 120 for conservative Protestant, and 225 for historically black congregations. The vast majority of congregations in the U.S. are Protestant (300,000), followed by Catholic and Orthodox (22,000), and non-Christian religious groups (12,000). The top five largest religious groups in the U.S. are: Roman Catholic (67 million), Southern Baptist (16 million), United Methodist (8 million), Mormon (6 million) and the Church of God in Christ—Pentecostal (5.5 million).

2. There are 251 seminaries in the U.S. and approximately 600,000 pastors. To prepare to become a pastor, many seminarians receive a Masters of Divinity degree which normally requires three to four years of academic and internship preparation. The average salary for pastors in the U.S. is $31,234 (this figure does not include the salaries of pastors of non-denominational congregations), and for Catholic priests, who normally receive free housing, the salary range is from $21,000 to 26,095.

3. The debate about whether or not Jesus was a good Jew is old and lengthy. Here we acknowledge that at times Jesus behaved like a good Jew, according to the religious precepts set down by religious leaders, and at times he did not act like a good Jew, judging by those same standards. Robinson (2005) puts this contradiction into perspective when he asserts that the reason the Gospels do not go into great detail about Jesus' conformity to Jewish rules was because they were written primarily for a Gentile audience. In an attempt at balance, he writes (p. 77): "… it is important to pay attention to the stories told about Jesus that do present him thinking and functioning as the Jew that he was." He adds that Jesus, still, was clearly a person who on many occasions went his own way: "But then it is all the more striking to find him on occasion breaking through his own cultural traditions, when he feels a higher claim to do the right thing called for by the situation."

INTRODUCTION

1. The 48th chapter of the Rule of St Benedict, by which the Trappist lives, states "for then are they monks in truth, if they live by the work of their hands." Whether at work or play, the monks are devoted to silence, personal poverty, and seclusion, maintaining as little contact with the outside world as possible. The group claims as one of their own perhaps the best known Catholic monk in the world, Thomas Merton (deceased), who was a prolific writer and world-renowned speaker, and whose book, *The Seven-Storey Mountain* is a devotional classic. Along with Merton, the Trappists are known for their ales and cheeses which are distilled and produced at the Chimay Brewery in Belgium. For ales, cheeses or caskets - you can travel to my neighborhood monastery, the New Melleray Abbey in Dubuque, Iowa, or visit it at www.newmelleray.org.

2. A friend, colleague, and Russian historian, Professor Greg Bruess, informs me that this technique of taking people to be executed was commonly used by the Red and White Armies in post-Revolution Russia not to actually kill someone, but to extort—i.e., your money or your life. Every Christmas, with his eighteen grandchildren gathered around, Grandpa listed off the items he was required to get for these thugs-posing-as-revolutionaries in order to stay alive: a pair of silk hose, two pillowcases, five pounds of sugar, and other scarce items. Grandpa never said whether or not he thought his captors meant to actually kill him. The tremble in his voice pretty much said it all.

3. The first TV football game was broadcast on Thanksgiving Day in 1956 by CBS.

4. Inflation that year stood at .04%!

5. For a popular expose, see the 11-part series "Class Matters" published in the New York Times, particularly Part 7: "When the Joneses Wear Jeans," (May 29, 2005). For a scholarly treatment on class and clothing, see Grant McCracken's (1988 *Culture and Consumption: New Approaches to the Symbolic Character of Consumer Goods and Activities;* In particular, see chapter four, "Clothing as Language: An Object Lesson in the Study of the Expressive Properties of Material Culture."

6. For another inspiring story along these lines, see Karen Samples article in *The Cincinnati Enquirer* (Sunday, February 18, 2001) titled: "Online and Off the Street: Homeless Man Reboots his Life;" and also see "Homeless Man Starts Mental Health Blog" (September 11, 2005), written by John Zicconi for the Vermont Press Bureau.

7. In the forty-eight contiguous states, the poverty level for a family of four is $21, 200 according to the *Federal Register*, Vol. 73, No. 15, January 23, 2008, pp. 3971–3972. The pretax income range for the U.S. middle class is between $35,000 and 75,000, according to factcheck.org. In truth, measuring class by income is a sticky wicket, particularly if the data is self-reported. It is not uncommon for a person living a middle-class lifestyle and making as little as $15,000 annually (say, an office receptionist) to report that he is middle class, and someone making as much as $100,000 a year (a lawyer) to report the same. For an interesting application of class to Christian voting behavior, see "Who Makes Up the Middle Class Vote? by Mark Martin (CBNNews.Com, May 1, 2008).

8. Not all have been as glowing about Niebuhr's *Christ and Culture* as Stackhouse. See, for example, John Howard Yoder's (1995) *Authentic Transformation*, Abingdon Press, and also "A Contested Classic: Critics Ask: Whose Christ? Which Culture?" by Peter R. Gathje in *The Christian Century*, June 19-26, 2008.

1. JESUS LANDLORD

1. Churchplantingresources.com states that one of the reasons brand new churches fail to survive is because the church planter (i.e., pastor) fails to understand the cost of maintaining a church plant: "Too many church planters don't know how a church plant works, nor have they

ever had to raise money. If a person can raise $50,000 before (building) the odds are the plant will thrive."

2. Bill Gates is a Congregationalist and Melinda Gates is a Catholic. Bill Gates has long said that, like Andrew Carnegie, he intends to give away most of his fortune. To his three children, he has willed 10 million USD apiece, approximately 5% of his $56 billion estate (Fortune Magazine, 2007). Where will the other 95% go? According to Wikipedia, the Bill & Melinda Gates Foundation had an endowment of 35.1 billion USD as of October 2008. The Foundation started by the Gates in 1994 is widely considered to be a leader in global philanthropy.

3. Some scholars believe that Jesus was illiterate; however, no hard evidence indicates whether or not Jesus could read. In his day, roughly 3-5% of the population could read. No other gospel besides Mark's calls Jesus a carpenter. In Matthew 13:55, Jesus is referred to as "the carpenter's son."

4. Jesus' poverty and low social position is mostly supported by two biblical references: Luke 2:7, the account of his birth in a manger, which indicates that his parents were too poor to afford better accommodations; and Luke 2:24, which records that Joseph offered birds (a poor person's offering) and not a lamb for the childbirth ceremony. Of Jesus' group, Horsley (1994, p. 136) writes: "The first followers of Jesus, like their master, were from the poor and hungry, not as the result of any renunciation of possessions but because they possessed nothing."

5. The idea of a "walking narrative" comes from De Certeau's chapter titled "Walking in the City." In this chapter, one of the most influential of all his writings, de Certeau describes the "city" as a "concept" defined by planners and the maneuvering of government officials, businesspeople, and institutional bodies. While these planners seek to strategically define the city as a unified whole, the reality is that the citizen walks about the city guided by his own aims and motives, tactfully not strategically. Thus the city consumer breaks the rules or "poaches" on the territory of others, sometimes ignoring the rules of the planners and sometimes reshaping them to meet his own personal desires and needs. Consequently, the person's life is influenced by the city planner's rules but not wholly determined by them. De Certeau's idea is, as I write later, descriptive of "Jesus Consumer's" life, someone who stuck to the rules at times but mostly went his own way, making it up as he went along, tailoring his response according to the person and the situation.

6. The Applied Research Institute of Jerusalem estimates that around 2.5 billion USD comes in every year from tourists who want to visit the places where Jesus walked.

7. Jesus' attitude about places was borne out of personal experience and, consequently, not unique to his thinking as much as it was distinctive of the culture in which he lived. Crossan (1998, p. 428) states that the apartments occupied by people in Jesus' day were not like the ones we moderns think of, writing: "People did not eat or live in them; they did not cook or defecate in them; they simply slept and stored in them." Crossan believes that the majority of early Christian converts did not live in private homes or villas but in the larger outdoor community, the neighborhood, a style of living which he describes as outdoor "communal living on a massive scale." This may help explain why so many of Jesus' references in his teachings were to nature. Robinson (2005) states that Jesus' appeal to nature to explain God outnumbered his references to the Torah and Jewish Law.

8. Crossan (1998, p. 286) writes: "… Christians did not invent asceticism, they adopted it from paganism," a point St. Francis, a Christian ascetic, readily acknowledged.

2. JESUS AMISH

1. See www.PADutch.Com for more details on this tragic story.
2. The argument for the connection between Anabaptism and revolutionary, coercive socialism is an old, but unconvincing one first articulated by Karl Kautsky, a central interpreter of Marxism following Friedrich Engels' death, in his essay (1919): "Communism in Central Europe in the Time of the Reformation." Modern writers who echo Kautsky's beliefs include Erik von Kuehnelt-Leddihn. In his book *Leftism*, Kuehnelt-Leddihn commenting on an early

Anabaptist treatise, the so-called Zurich Doctrines, states that prohibitions against private property "were obeyed in the most uncompromising and radical form. Government offices, oaths and the use of arms were strictly outlawed. Nobody owned property. The stranger who asked for Baptism had to surrender all his earthly goods to the community but in the case of excommunication or banishment nothing was returned to him. Family life, which cannot be imagined without property, was replaced with a different order. The marriages, without consultation of the partners, were decreed and blessed by the Servants of the Word. The children soon after their birth were handed over to wet nurses and later placed in the common school house. Dressed and fed in an identical way, the adults lived according to their occupation in larger households under the supervision of a Servant of Necessity. The whole life moved, day in day out, within the narrowest limits. Any manifestation of personal independence or freedom led to banishment which meant to bottomless misery." Most agree that Kautsky's observations conform far better to Marxist theory than historical fact.

3. Amish tourism in Ohio alone brings in about 2.5 billion USD annually and in Philadelphia, 8.3 million tourists spend more than $3.2 billion USD every year visiting Amish country.

4. These five instructions come from the Gospel of Luke, chapter 10. Here are listed other citations from the synoptic gospels that support these consumption codes: The Gospels of *Matthew* (7, 11: 7-8, 10: 9-12, 6: 19-21, and 19: 23-25); *Mark* (8: 34-37); and *Luke* (7: 25, 22: 35-36, 12: 15-21, 18: 28; 30, 12: 15-21, 14: 33). The so-called Lord's Prayer or "Our Father" expresses the give-and-take generosity Jesus intended for people in the words: "forgive us our trespasses as we forgive those who trespass against us." While this part of the prayer has been traditionally interpreted as applying to non-monetary trespasses, Robinson (2005, 171) points out that they were directed also at financial indebtedness and should be interpreted: "Cancel our debts for us, as we too have canceled for those in debt to us."

5. An assortment of Christian leaders through the ages have viewed Jesus' teachings as less than compelling by assigning a secondary importance to them relative to Paul's letters. For example, Luther wrote: " Therefore St. Paul's Epistles are more a Gospel than Matthew, Mark and Luke." C.S. Lewis wrote: "The Gospel is not in the gospels" (but in the Epistles). And Billy Graham famously wrote in a widely circulated tract: "Jesus came to do three days work, to die, be buried, and raised from the dead. Jesus came not primarily to preach the Gospel."

6. This may still be true. A 2007 study reported by the Hartford Institute for Religion Research suggests that conservative Protestant churches still fall short when it comes to the number of community services they sponsor. In the report, the average number of community services per five different Christian groups were as follows: Catholic—7.4, Mainline Protestant—5.4, Conservative Protestant—2.9, Historical Black Churches—6.9, Other—4.8, and All—4.5.

7. I use the word "roots" because these two sources in particular— Q and Mark— are believed by most scholars to have been extensively used referentially by the writers of the Gospels of Matthew, Luke, and John whose accounts were written some 50-70 years after Q and Mark. James Robinson (2005) writes: "… the Gospel of Matthew was rooted in the Q community. The Sayings Gospel Q itself is not in the New Testament, but everything is Q nonetheless in the New Testament because it is in Matthew and Luke." Crossan (1998, p. 149) concurs, writing about the relationship of the very earliest gospels to the later ones: "the Q Gospel and Mark are absorbed massively into Matthew and Luke."

8. Below is a sampling of other writing by Tertullian that reference consumer rules for (mostly women) Christians in the third century. I have italicized specific consumption laws:

For those women sin against God when they rub their skin with *ointments*, stain their cheeks with *rouge*, and make their eyes prominent with antimony. To them, I suppose, the artistic skill of God is displeasing (circa 198 AD).

Whatever is born is the work of God. So whatever is plastered on, is the devil's work.... How unworthy of the Christian name it is to wear a fictitious *face*—you on whom simplicity in every form is enjoined! You, to whom lying with the tongue is not lawful, are lying in appearance (circa 198 AD).

What purpose, again, does all the labor spent in arranging the *hair* render to salvation? Why is no rest allowed to your hair? First, it must be bound, then loosed, then cultivated, then thinned out? Some are anxious to force their hair into curls (circa 198 AD).

I will then see whether you will rise [at the resurrection] with your *ceruse* and *rouge* and *saffron*—and in all that parade of *headgear*. I will then see whether it will be women thus decked out whom the angels carry up to meet Christ in the air! If these things are now good, and of God, they will then also present themselves to the rising bodies (circa 198 AD).

Concerning modesty of dress and embellishments, indeed, the commandment of Peter is likewise plain, restraining as he does with the same mouth . . . the glory of *garments*, the pride of *gold*, and the showy elaboration of the *hair* (circa 198 AD).

First, then, blessed sisters, take heed that you do not admit to your use flashy and sluttish garbs and *clothing* (circa 198 AD).

This [male] sex of ours acknowledges to itself deceptive trickeries of form peculiarly its own. I am referring to things such as . . . arranging the *hair*, and disguising its hoariness by *dyes* (circa 198 AD).

What will I say of the fact that these [young women] of ours confess their change of age even by their garb! As soon as they have understood themselves to be women,... they lay aside their former selves. They change their *hair* and fasten their hair with more wanton *pins*, professing obvious womanhood with their hair parted from the front. The next thing, they consult the mirror to aid their beauty. They thin down their over-exacting *face* with washing. Perhaps they even dress it up with *cosmetics*. They toss their mantle about them with an air, fit tightly into the multiform *shoe*, and carry down more ample *appliances* to the baths (circa 207 AD).

    9. Some writers argue that the term "Protestant Sectarian" is a misnomer. Walter Klaassen's book titled: *Anabaptism: Neither Protestant nor Catholic*," builds support for this position. George (1988, p. 269) suggests that the Anabaptists could not be technically called Protestant as they rejected the *sine qua non* of Luther's theology: "Menno [Simons], and Anabaptists generally, did not accept Luther's forensic doctrine of justification by faith alone because they saw it as an impediment to the true doctrine of a 'lively' faith which issues in holy living."

    10. The Global Anabaptist Mennonite Encyclopedia Online states: "Luther disputed theologically with the Anabaptists only in literary form, and principally in four writings: (1) his booklet Von der Wiedertaufe an zwei Pfarrherrn of 1528 (WA 26, 137ff.); (2) the foreword to the book by Justus Menius, Der Wiedertäufer Lehre und Geheimnis of 1530 (WA 30, 2, 209ff.); (3) his Von den Schleichern und Winkelpredigern of 1532 (WA 30, 3, 510ff.); and (4) his sermons of 2, 9, 16, and 23 February 1528 (WA 27), as well as in the Kirchenpostille of 1523 for the Gospel on the third Sunday after Epiphany (WA 17, 2, 72 ff.), also separately published under the title Von der Kinder Tauf und fremdem Glauben in the introduction to Urbanus Rhegius' Widerlegung des Bekenntnisses der Münsterischen neuen Valentinianer und Donatisten und zur Neuen Zeitung von den Wiedertäufern zu Münster 1535 (WA 38, 336ff.)."

    11. Representative of Bonhoeffer's radical stance is this passage taken from *The Cost of Discipleship:* "The life of discipleship can only be maintained so long as nothing is allowed to come between Christ and ourselves, neither the law, nor personal piety, nor even the world. The disciple looks always only to his master, never to Christ AND the law, Christ AND religion, Christ AND the world. Only by following Christ alone can he preserve a single eye."

    12. See Vineyard.org for more information.

    13. What specific consumer acts do today's U.S. Christian churches prohibit? The results of a survey of characteristics of American congregations by faith group (visit www.uscongregations.org) lists nine possible prohibitions, seven of which are consumer prohi-

bition (italicized and listed here from most to least often prohibited). They include: homosexuality, cohabitation before marriage, *gambling, alcohol, smoking, financial contributions to certain groups, dancing, foods, dress, hairstyle,* and *make-up.* The findings reflect that conservative Protestant churches are the strictest prescribing on average 3.2 prohibitions, followed by Historic Black Churches (2.9), Catholics (1.5) and Mainline Protestants (1.1). My own informal survey of denominational and organizational Web sites revealed the following: The National Association of Evangelicals (NAE) Web site lists no consumer prohibitions for their members (see www.nae.net). The Southern Baptist Convention Web site lists no consumer prohibitions. It does endorse prohibitions against homosexuality and abortion, but not birth control. The Vineyard Ministries Web site lists no consumer prohibitions. Representative universities and colleges do list some prohibitions for their students. For example, Oral Roberts University (ORU) (representative of a charismatic church campus whose rules would, presumably be prescriptive for its member constituents), in a student guideline publication titled: "Ties and Skirts: Addressing the Issue" (ORU: Alumni Foundation), states that "all students are required to sign a pledge stating they will live according to the university's honor code, which prohibits lying, cursing, *smoking, drinking, gambling* and a range of sexual acts including homosexual behavior." Wikipedia reports that "in early 2004, the student dress code at ORU was relaxed for the first time in forty years and described as *business casual.* For most of the school's history men were required to wear *button-down shirts and ties* while women were required to wear *skirts* (an exception for winter months was added in 2000). In 2006 campus-wide dress code rules were eased even further, allowing students to wear *jeans* to class and dress even more casually in non-academic settings. Beginning in 2009, men are allowed to have neatly trimmed *facial hair.* Restrictions on men concerning *hair length and earrings* remain." Bob Jones University (representative of a fundamentalist church campus) states in the 2005-06 Day Student Handbook: "Loyalty to Christ results in separated living. Dishonesty, lewdness, sensual behavior, adultery, homosexuality, sexual perversion of any kind, pornography, illegal use of drugs, and drunkenness—all are clearly condemned by God's word and prohibited here. Grounds for immediate dismissal include stealing, immorality (including sexual relations between unmarried students), possession of hard-core pornography, use of *alcohol* or drugs, and participating in a public demonstration for a cause the University opposes. Similar "moral failures" are grounds for terminating the employment of faculty and staff." R. Judson Carlberg of Gordon College (representative of an evangelical church campus) writes in "The Future of Religious Colleges: The Evangelical Vision from Fundamentalist Isolation to Respected Voice," (see www.collegenews.org): "Contemporary colleges within the evangelical camp tend to define their communities far differently than they did 50 years ago. At that time, what was *not* allowed, (smoking, drinking alcohol, dancing, playing cards, attending movies or theater) seemed far more important. While selected prohibitions still are honored by some in the tradition, these rules and restrictions are less important as a means of defining evangelicals today." Of the *entertainment business,* Carlberg writes: "Students (in evangelical colleges) today are encouraged to enter the entertainment and media fields to become "salt and light" in professions which are still perceived to be hostile to Christianity in general and to evangelicals in particular."

14. The vow of renunciation of all private property was introduced in 1260. According to the Catholic Encyclopedia: "The vow of poverty may generally be defined as the promise made to God of a certain constant renunciation of temporal goods, in order to follow Christ. The object of the vow of poverty is anything visible, material, appreciable at a money value. The solemn vow by common law has the following special characteristics: it extends to all property and rights; it renders one incapable of possessing property, and therefore of transferring it; it makes all gifts or legacies which a religious receives, as well as the fruits of his own work, the property of the monastery; and in case property is inherited, the monastery succeeds in place of the professed religious ...." Contrary to popular opinion, not all priests take the vow of poverty.

15. Catholic beliefs about private property are stated in *The Catholic Encyclopedia*: "Jesus Christ did not condemn the possession of worldly goods, or even of great wealth; for He himself had rich friends. Patristic tradition condemns the opponents of private property...."

16. The only *official* statement concerning the vices that I was able to locate was that issued by Pope Innocent in 1650 against smoking in St. Peter's Cathedral in Rome. The Catholic

Church is not unaware of the negative outcomes of partaking in so-called "vices." For example, regarding gambling, the *Catechism of the Catholic Church* instructs: "Games of chance (card games, etc.) or wagering are not in themselves contrary to justice. They become morally unacceptable when they deprive someone of what is necessary to provide for his needs and those of others (or when) the passion of gambling risks becoming an enslavement." Along with certain places, the Catholic Church encourages the prohibition of some behaviors during certain times; for example, smoking, drinking, and gambling along with other consumption behaviors are strongly discouraged during Lent.

17. Hitler was expelled from school at the age of 8 for smoking and continued smoking until the age of 30. Later in life he became a vegetarian and led the first public anti-smoking campaign in modern times.

18. Intellectuals are notoriously critical of consumerism, particularly the shopping experience. See for example Mitroff and Bennis (1989) who write about shopping malls, which they call "the unreality industry," that they "deliberately manufacture falsehood;" or Langman (1992) who sees the mall as an instrument of dehumanization, an enslaver of people, and a master manipulator that distorts the person's true self. And of course we shouldn't' forget Marx who believed that the capitalist economy leads to the "fetishization" of goods.

3. JESUS CONTRACTOR

1. Here is a sampling of other consumer teachings set down in the Epistles:

Every man who has something on his head while praying or prophesying, disgraces his head. But every woman who has her *head uncovered* while praying or prophesying, disgraces her head... (1 Corinthians 11:4-5).

Likewise, I want women to adorn themselves with *proper clothing*, modestly and discreetly, not with *braided hair and gold or pearls or costly garments*; but rather by means of good works, as befits women making a claim to godliness (1 Timothy 2:9-10).

Whose adorning let it not be that outward adorning of plaiting the *hair*, and of wearing of *gold*, or of putting on of a*pparel*; But let it be the hidden man of the heart, in that which is not corruptible, even the ornament of a meek and quiet spirit, which is in the sight of God of great price (1 Peter 3:3-4).

Does not even nature itself teach you that if a man has *long hair*, it is a dishonor to him, but if a woman has long hair, it is a glory to her? For her hair is given to her for a covering (1 Corinthians 11:14-15).

2. A *short* list of researchers who have offered empirical and theoretical support for the idea that humans are "not literal" include: William James, John R. Anderson, Alan Baddeley, Albert Bandura, Frederic Bartlett, Aaron T. Beck, Margaret Boden, Donald Broadbent, Jerome Bruner, Gordon H. Bower, Fergus Craik, Kenneth Craik, Noam Chomsky, Hermann Ebbinghaus, Albert Ellis, Keith Holyoak, Daniel Kahneman, Elizabeth Loftus, Jean Piaget, Steven Pinker, Michael Posner, George Armitage Miller, Ulrich Neisser, Roger Shepard, Elizabeth Spelke, George Sperling, Saul Sternberg, Endel Tulvin, Anne Treisman, and Ken Nakayama.

3. For more details, see "The Story behind SB's Dog, Cat, and Rat Man" by Emilia Dellimonico in the May 21, 2008 edition of *The Bottom Line,* a newspaper published by Associated Students UC Santa Barbara (www.thebottomline.as.ucsb.edu).

4. For more information see McCracken (1988), in particular chapter five: "Meaning Manufacture and Movement in the World of Goods.

5. Here, for example, are the results of a study commissioned by a conservative Christian sect who prescribe that their female members wear head coverings. The study examines how

this consumer rule, the "head covering rule," changed over time as practiced in one of the church's high schools. The findings are summarized below:

> *1943:* Dress length should be half-way between the ankles and knees, or lower. Dresses should have full sleeves and capes. Girls should wear black stockings. No loud colors or large prints are allowed. Prayer caps with ties be worn at all times.
> *1949:* Dresses must extend 3" below the knee, or lower for freshmen and sophomores, one-third the way down from the knees or lower for juniors and seniors.
> *1954:* Prayer cap ties are no longer required. (According to eyewitnesses, when this change was announced at a school assembly, all of the girls immediately ripped the ties off of their caps.)
> *1961:* Teachers were allowed to remove their prayer cap strings.
> *1963:* Requirement for black stockings removed from dress code.
> *1968:* Dresses only need to cover one's knees.
> *1971:* Girls allowed to remove prayer caps during sports activities.
> *1972:* Girls allowed to wear their hair down if they keep it in a ponytail or pigtail. Headcoverings no longer required on the senior trip.
> *1978:* Headcoverings only required during school hours while on campus. Girls may have their hair down, unbound. (Of 99 senior girls, only 11 choose to have their hair up in their school pictures.)
> *1980:* Girls no longer are required to wear a headcovering. Of 84 senior girls, only 18 wear headcoverings and only 10 have their hair up in their senior pictures. Most headcoverings are of the chapel veil or doilie type instead of the traditional prayer cap.
> *1984:* Female teachers no longer required to wear headcoverings.
> *1986:* Of 77 senior girls, only one wears a headcovering in her senior picture. Not one has their hair up. Only one female teacher wears a headcovering.

What would these researchers have us conclude? It is that, because the head covering rule is not as adhered to today as in the past, this particular denomination is in a moral freefall (the researchers refer to the trend away from head covering as evidence of a "drift away from Biblical standards." This raises a question about the moral drift of millions of female Christians who not only do not wear head coverings but have never been even remotely aware that this is what is required to meet biblical standards. This kind of strict attention to consumer rules is viewed by most Christians as peculiar, and yet it was not (nor is not, as we read later) unique to this group. In fact, strict adherence to consumer rules is a significant part of Christian history.

6. Indeed, the idea—often proposed by consumer radicals— that godless societies are more likely than God-fearing ones to devolve into lawlessness and immorality is questionable, according to the book, *Society without God: What the least religious nations can teach us about contentment*, written by sociologist Phil Zuckerman (2008). Today, Zuckerman writes, two of the least religious countries in the world - Denmark and Sweden - are some of the most law-abiding and moral in the world, if they are to be judged by their strong economies, low crime rates, and high standards of social equality. Yet Danes and Swedes, according to Zuckerman's research are largely unconcerned and even incurious about faith, God, and the meaning of their lives. (A controversial position that you can weigh-in on by visiting www.balloon-juice.com.).

4. JESUS ESPRESSO

1. The coffee drinkers used here, like Wendy, were initially part of a study conducted by Susan Fournier and Julie Yao's, titled: "Reviving brand loyalty: A reconceptualization with the framework of consumer-brand relationships," and found in the *International Journal of Research in Marketing*, 14, (1997): 451-472. Dunkin' Donuts serves approximately 2.7 million customers per day. In recent years, Dunkin' Donuts has annually sold more coffee products

than donuts and consequently, the organization has added to its merchandise branded bulk coffee and a full line of espresso drinks. It competes directly with Starbucks who currently owns approximately three times as many stores (over 15,000) as Dunkin' Donuts (just under 6,000).

2. Garage sales in the U.S. began in the 1950s and 60s as American suburbanites became more affluent, leading many to accumulate in excess. By the 1970s, the American garage sale had become a permanent fixture in the American way of life. According to www.family.com, there are anywhere from 6.5 million to 9 million garage sales a year in the U.S. generating $1.5 to 2 million USD. In 2006, the Department of Revenue estimated that garage sales in the state of Washington alone took in $41 million USD (www.seattlepi.com). For academic research on U.S. garage sales and flea markets, see John Sherry (1990). "A Sociocultural Analysis of a Midwestern American Flea Market," *Journal of Consumer Research*, 17 (1): 13-30; and Russell Belk, Melanie Wallendorf, and John Sherry (1989). The Sacred and Profane in Consumer Behavior: Theodicy on the Odyssey, *Journal of Consumer Research* 16 (1): 1-38.

3. For a positive spin to spiraling shopping, see Nissanoff, Dan (2006). FutureShop : How the New Auction Culture Will Revolutionize the Way We Buy, Sell and Get the Things We Really Want, Penguin Press. Nissandoff's central argument is that because of online auctions sites, such as eBay, there is a new level of "liquidity (i.e. buying and selling) that is moving America from an "accumulation nation" of hoarders to one where possessions are quickly and constantly replaced with ever better items (i.e., a "better is more" argument.) Consumptianity argues instead that, to make our consumption experience better requires contemplation and thoughtfulness on the part of the consumer, not speed and liquidity on the part of our systems of distribution.

4. Actually, two dollars for a cup of coffee is a pretty good deal. According to a 2008 Mercer's Cost of Living Survey, the most expensive coffee in the world is found in Moscow at $10.19 (this is standard cup of coffee, not an espresso drink which would be far more expensive). In other cities you pay: $6.77 (Paris), $6.22 (Athens), and $3.75 (New York City. The cheapest cup of (big city) coffee is served in Buenos Aires and Johannesburg for $2.36. On the supply side, Starbucks coffee costs about $1,280 per barrel.

5. JESUS CORPORATE

1. Animosity between these parties is well documented. *First, Luther*: Luther encouraged true Christians to murder Catholic bishops and destroy their property (see Against the Falsely Called *Spiritual Order of the Pope and the Bishops*), He writes: "It were better that every bishop were murdered, every [monastery or convent] rooted out, that one soul should be destroyed ... But if they will not hear God's Word, but rage and rave with bannings and burnings, killings and every evil, what do they better deserve than a strong uprising which will sweep them from the earth? And we would smile did it happen. ... All who contribute body, goods and honor that the rule of the bishops may be destroyed are God's dear children and true Christians." Of the Anabaptists, Luther held that those who believed water baptism was only a symbol and not a sacrament (means of grace) were not saved, and in 1527, he wrote ...." the Anabaptists [reject] baptism, and therefore they cannot efficiently baptize ... (Table Talk—p. 180). *Second, the Catholic Church*, as articulated by Pope St. Leo X: "Wherefore, since outside the Catholic Church there is nothing perfect, nothing undefiled, the Apostle declaring that "all that is not of faith is sin" (Romans 14:23), we are in no way likened with those who are divided from the unity of the Body of Christ; we are joined in no communion." *Third, the Anabaptists*, as stated in Article IV of the Schleitheim Confession: "From this we should learn that everything which is not united with our God and Christ cannot be other than an abomination which we should shun and flee from. By this is meant all Catholic and Protestant works and church services, meetings and church attendance, drinking houses, civic affairs, the oaths sworn in unbelief and other things of that kind, which are highly regarded by the world and yet are carried on in flat contradiction to the command of God, in accordance with all the unrighteousness which is in the world." Of the three groups, the Anabaptists fared the worst at the hands of

both Protestant and Catholic princes, in part due to their stance of nonresistance and nonviolence. Esteemed Anabaptist historian, Harold S. Bender (1944) writes: "The dreadful severity of the persecution of the Anabaptist movement in the years 1527-60 not only in Switzerland, South Germany, and Thuringia, but in all the Austrian lands as well as in the Low Countries, testifies to the power of the movement and the desperate haste with which Catholic, Lutheran, and Zwinglian authorities alike strove to throttle it before it should be too late. The notorious decree issued in 1529 by the Diet of Spires (the same diet which protested the restriction of evangelical liberties) summarily passed the sentence of death upon all Anabaptists, ordering that "every Anabaptist and rebaptized person of either sex should be put to death by fire, sword, or some other way." Repeatedly in subsequent sessions of the imperial diet this decree was reinvoked and intensified; and as late as 1551 the Diet of Augsburg issued a decree ordering that judges and jurors who had scruples against pronouncing the death sentence on Anabaptists be removed from office and punished by heavy fines and imprisonment."

2. With so many small struggling churches, does Paul's model make sense too? Yes, of course. Paul's model is a brilliant one that should not be ignored or discarded any more than Jesus' mission instructions or his discipleship model of organization. I simply maintain here that in a consumer culture where innovation and change is valued, and where permanency and loyalty are not, a society in which the survival of the Church and Christianity is no more threatened than that of Rice Krispies or Midas Muffler, both small and struggling churches as well as larger, thriving congregations stand to also benefit from the organizational model implicit in Jesus' disciple group. For the small church, tightly focused projects with measurable goals and outcomes permits even the tiniest of churches to have a significant impact. For larger churches, small ad-hoc mission groups focused on one or two measurable goals and outcomes nurtures close, one-on-one relationships and coordination. In other words, Jesus' model permits small churches, even those that struggle to make ends meet, to experience the kind of social impact and accomplishment previously accomplished by large congregations with large budgets, and it allows large churches to continue their influence while simultaneously helping nurture an intimate group dynamic so cherished in small congregations and often absent in large ones.

References

Belk, Russell W. (2006). *Research in Consumer Behavior, Vol. 10*, editor, Oxford: Elsevier Science, Ltd.
Belk, Russell W. (2000). *Research in Consumer Behavior, Vol. 9*, Stamford, CT: JAI Press, co-editor with Janeen Arnold Costa and John Schouten.
Belk, Russell W. (1997). Resea*rch in Consumer Behavior, Vol. 8*, Greenwich, CT: JAI Press, editor.
Belk, Russell W. (1989). "Extended Self and Extending Paradigmatic Perspective," *Journal of Consumer Research*, 15 (1, June), 129-132.
Belk, Russell W., Melanie Wallendorf and John Sherry (1989). "The Sacred and the Profane in Consumer Behavior: Theodicy on the Odyssey," *Journal of Consumer Research*.
Belk, Russell W., David Tse and Nan Zhou (1989). "Becoming a Consumer Society: A Longitudinal and Cross-Cultural Content Analysis of Print Advertisements from Hong Kong, People's Republic of China and Taiwan," Journal of Consumer Research, 15 (4, March), 457-472.
Bender, Harold. (1944). The Anabaptist Vision," Scottsdale, PA: Herald Press.
Berger, Peter L. and Thomas Luckmann (1967). *The Social Construction of Behavior,* New York: Anchor Books.
Bonhoeffer, D. (1948). The Cost of Discipleship, Touchstone Press.
Borg, Marcus J. (1994). *Jesus in Contemporary Scholarship,* Valley Forge, PA: Trinity Press.
Bourdieu, Pierre (1990). *The Logic of Practice*, Cambridge: Polity Press.
Braudel, Fernand (1979). *The Perspective of the World*, New York: Harper & Row.
Braudel, Fernand (1992). *The Structures of Every Day Life*, Berkeley, CA: University of California Press
Brown, Peter (1982). "Response" (to Robert M. Grant's "The Problem of Miraculous Feedings in the Graeco-Roman World"). In Protocol of the Forty-Second Colloquy (March 14, 1982), pp. 16-24. Berkeley: Center for Hermeneutical Studies in Hellenistic and Modern Culture (The Graduate Theological Union and the University of California at Berkeley).
Brown, Raymond E. (1982). *The Gospel of Thomas and St. John's Gospel*, NTS 9: 155-177.
Bruner, J. S. & Goodman, C. C. (1947). Value and need as organizing factors in perception. *Journal of Abnormal Social Psychology*, 42, 33-44.
Carroll, James (2001). *Constantine's Sword: The Church and the Jews*, New York: Houghton Mifflin and Company.
Combs, Arthur W. and Snygg, Donald (1949), *Individual Behavior: A New Frame of Reference for Psychology*. New York, Harper & Brothers.
Cox, W. Michael and Alm, Richard. *New York Times:* "How Americans Spend their Money," Sunday February 10, 2008.

References

Crossan, John Dominique (1991). *The Historical Jesus: The Life of a Mediterranean Jewish Peasant*, San Francisco, CA: HarperSanFrancisco.

Crossan, John Dominique (1999). *The Birth of Christianity: Discovering what Happened in the Years Immediately after the Execution of Jesus*, San Francisco, CA" HarperCollins.

Csikszentmihalyi, Mihaly and Eugene Rochberg-Halton (1981). *The Meaning of Things: Domestic Symbols and Self*, Cambridge: Cambridge University Press.

De Certeau, Michel (1984). *The Practice of Everyday Life*, Berkeley, CA: University of California Press.

De Certeau, Michel; Luce Giard and Pierre Mayol (1998). *The Practice of Everyday Life, Volume 2: Living and Cooking*, Minneapolis, MN: University of Minnesota Press.

De Grazia, V. (1981). *Culture of Consent: Mass Organization of Leisure in Fascist Italy*, NY: Cambridge University Press.

De Grazia, V. and Furlough, E. (1996). *The Sex of Things: Gender and Consumption in Historical Perspective*, Berkeley, CA: University of California Press.

Delanda, Manuel (2006). A New Philosophy of Society: Assemblage Theory and Social Complexity, London: Continuum Books.

Diderot, Denis (1964). "Regrets on Parting with My Old Dressing Gown," in *Rameau's Nephew and Other Works*, New York: Bobbs-Merrill.

Dobrowolski, K. (1971). "Peasant Traditional Culture." In Peasants and Peasant Society: Selected Readings, edited by Teodor Shanin, pp. 277-298. Baltimore, MD: Penguin Books.

Ehrenreich, Barbara. (2001) *Nickel and Dimed*, New York: Henry Holt and Company.

Foucault, Michel (1974). The Order of Things: An Archeology of the Human Science, London: Tavistock.

Fournier, S. and Yao, J. (1997). "Reviving Brand Loyalty: A Reconceptualization with the Framework of Consumer-Brand Relationships," International Journal of Research in Marketing, 14: 451-472.

Freud, Sigmund (1927). *The Future of an Illusion*, Vienna: Liveright Publishing Corporation.

Freud, Sigmund (1930). *Civilization and its Discontents*, London: Hogarth Press.

Fromm, Erich (1941). *Escape from Freedom*, London: Routledge.

Giddens, Anthony. (1979). *Central Problems in Social Theory*, Berkeley, CA: University of California Press.

Giddens, Anthony (1986). *The Constitution of Society*, Berkeley, CA: University of California Press.

Gilles, Deleuze 1991. *Empiricism and Subjectivity,* New York: Columbia University Press.

George, T. (1988). Theology of the Reformers. (Nashville: Broadman).

Goffman, Erving (1967). Interaction Rituals: Essays on Face-to-Face Behavior, New York: Pantheon Books.

Goodman, M. (1987). *The Ruling Class of Judaea: The Origins of the Jewish Revolt Against Rome, A.D. 66-70*. Cambridge, UK: Cambridge University Press.

Hankiss, Elemer (2006). The Toothpaste of Immortality: Self-Construction in the Consumer Age, Baltimore, MD: The Johns Hopkins Press.

Heath, Joseph and Potter, Andrew. (2004). *The Rebel Sell*, NY: Harper Perennial.

Hirschman, Elizabeth C. and Morris Holbrook, Eds., (1981). *Symbolic Consumer Behavior*, Ann Arbor, MI: Association for Consumer Research.

Horsley, G. (1994). "The Historical Jesus and Archaeology of the Galilee: Questions from Historical Jesus Research to Archaeologists." In Society of Biblical Literature 1994 Seminar Papers, ed. By E. H. Lovering, Jr., pp. 91-135. 130th annual meetings, November 19-22, 1994, Chicago. Atlanta: Scholars Press.

Izard, C., Kagan, J., & Zajonc, R. (Eds.). (1984). Emotions, cognition, and behavior. Cambridge, UK: Cambridge University Press.

James, W. (1890). *The Principles of Psychology*, Dover Publications.

Jaroslav Pelikan. (1973) *The Christian Tradition: A History of the Development of Doctrine – Volume 1: The Emergence of the Catholic Tradition 100–600.*

Klinghoffer, David (2005). *Why the Jews Rejected Jesus*, New York: Doubleday.

Klassen, Michael L. (2007). *Bad Religion: The Psychology of Religious Misbehavior*, Lanham, MD: Rowman and Littlefield/University Press of America.

Lasn, Kalle. (2000). *Culture Jam: The Uncooling of America*, NY: HarperCollins.
Levy, Sidney (1981). Interpreting Consumer Mythology: A Structural Approach to Consumer Behavior," *Journal of Marketing*, 45, (Summer), 49-61.
McCracken, Grant (1988). *Culture and Consumption: New Approaches to the Symbolic Character of Consumer Goods and Activities,* Bloomington, IN: Indiana University Press.
Malina, Bruce and R.L. Rohrbaugh (1992). *Social Science Commentary on the Synoptic Gospels.* Minneapolis, MN: Fortress Press.
Marks, John. *Reasons to Believe: One Man's Journey among the Evangelicals and the Faith He Left Behind.* New York: HarperCollins, 2008.
Mick, David G. (1986). Consumer Research and Semiotics: Exploring the Morphology of Signs, Symbols, and Significance," *Journal of Consumer Research*, 13 (2 September), 196-213.
Niebuhr, H. Richard (1951). *Christ and Culture*, New York: Harper & Brothers.
Nissanoff, D. (2006). *FutureShop: How the new auction culture will revolutionize the way we buy, sell and get the things we really want,*" Penguin.
Perry, Charles. (2004). The Haight-Ashbury: A History (Reprint ed.), SF: Wenner Books.
Pollay, Richard W. (1986). "The Distorted Mirror: Reflections on the Unintended Consequences of Advertising," *Journal of Marketing,* 50 (2 April), 18-36.
Reed, Jonathan L. (1992). *The Population of Capernaum.* Occasional Papers of the Institute for Antiquity and Christianity, 24. Claremont, CA: Institute for Antiquity and Christianity.
Robinson, James M. (2005). *The Gospel of Jesus*, San Francisco, CA: Harper.
Rook, Dennis (1985). "The Ritual Dimension of Consumer Behavior," *Journal of Consumer Research,* 12 (3 December), 251-264.
Rubin, Jerry (1970). *Do It!*, NY: Simon and Schuster.
Sherry, John. (1990). "A Sociocultural Analysis of a Midwestern American Flea Market," *Journal of Consumer Research*, 17 (1): 13-30.
Stearns, Peter N. (1997). *Fat History: Bodies and Beauty in the Modern* West, NY: New York University Press.
Stearns, Peter N. (2006). Consumerism in World History: The Global Transformation of Desire, 2nd Edition, New York: Routledge.
Taleb, Nassim N. (2005, second edition). Fooled by Randomness: The Hidden Role of Chance in Life and in the Markets, New York: Random House.
Tilley, Charles (2002). *Stories, Identities and Political Change*, Lanham, MD: Rowman & Littlefield.
Trueblood, E. (1964). *The Humor of Christ*, New York: Harper & Row.
Wallis, Jim. (2005).*God's Politics: Why the Right Gets it Wrong and the Left Doesn't Get it,* HarperOne.
Weber, Max (1964). *The Theory of Social and Economic Organizations*, New York: Free Press of Glencoe.
Weber, Max (1958). The Protestant Ethic and the Spirit of Capitalism, New York: Scribner.
Wilentz, Sean. (2008). *The Age of Reagan: A History, 1974-2008*, NY: HarperCollins.
Zuckerman, P. (2008). *Society without God: What the least religious countries in the world can teach us about contentment."*

About the Author

Michael L. Klassen, Ph.D., a former pastor, is a university professor, psychologist, and the author of over sixty journal articles on business. This is his fourth book. Dr. Klassen has spoken to audiences and classrooms worldwide. His research has been featured on *ABC 20/20* and *NBC News Magazine—Europe/Asia,* and he has appeared on *Dateline NBC*. He and his wife live in Cedar Falls, and they have three grown children.

www.ingramcontent.com/pod-product-compliance
Lightning Source LLC
Chambersburg PA
CBHW052133300426
44116CB00010B/1878